mindful mamma

About the Author

Sophie Fletcher is a clinical hypnotherapist and doula and has been teaching simple mindfulness to new parents since 2006. She has a Master's degree in Language and Culture with a special interest in the psychology of language. Since 2004 Sophie has been specialising in hypnotherapy and mindfulness for birth and parenting and is an expert in her field – thousands of couples have read her bestselling book *Mindful Hypnobirthing* or have been through her Mindful Hypnobirthing programme. Sophie trains midwives, psychologists, doctors and other therapists in this approach and has lectured at universities on the topic of mindfulness and hypnosis for perinatal care and women's health and wellbeing. She lives in Grantham, Lincolnshire with her husband and two teenage boys.

If you want to know more about Sophie's work, or get in touch, join her social media community on the Facebook page Mindful Mamma Hypnobirthing or on Instagram @sophiefletcher_author, where you can find out tips and where she is giving talks and running workshops.

mindful mamma

Mindfulness and Hypnosis
Techniques for a Calm and
Confident First Year

Sophie Fletcher

Vermilion
LONDON

1 3 5 7 9 10 8 6 4 2

Vermilion, an imprint of Ebury Publishing,
20 Vauxhall Bridge Road,
London SW1V 2SA

Vermi' ... anies
whos ... .com

www.penguin.co.uk

A CIP catalogue record for this book is available from
the British Library

ISBN 9781785042812

Typeset in 10.2/15 pt Quire Sans Pro
by Integra Software Services Pvt. Ltd, Pondicherry

Printed and bound in Great Britain by Clays Ltd, Elcograf S.p.A.

Penguin Random House is committed to a sustainable
future for our business, our readers and our planet.
This book is made from Forest Stewardship Council®
certified paper.

The information in this book has been compiled by way of general guidance in
relation to the specific subjects addressed. It is not a substitute and not to be
relied on for medical, healthcare, pharmaceutical or other professional advice
on specific circumstances and in specific locations. Please consult your GP
before changing, stopping or starting any medical treatment. So far as the
author is aware the information given is correct and up to date as at November
2019. Practice, laws and regulations all change, and the reader should obtain up
to date professional advice on any such issues. The author and publishers
disclaim, as far as the law allows, any liability arising directly or indirectly from
the use, or misuse, of the information contained in this book.

To Gordon, Fin and Rory

I am glad that you chose me.
(And for teaching me about the miraculous
properties of tea and a hug.)

In a family, just one person needs to practise mindfulness for the rest of the family to be mindful

Thich Nhat Hanh

Contents

Part Four: Embracing the Mother in You

Gender Identity and the Word 'Mother'

For the purpose of this book I have used the words 'mother', 'mothering', 'parent', 'parenting' and 'partner' interchangeably. Virtually all research in this area is based on the 'mother' and baby. However, I recognise that if you do not identify as female, this may feel uncomfortable in places. If you are interested in listening to any of the tracks without the word mother in, please contact Sophie Fletcher directly. The worksheets that accompany this book are available to download in different formats as well.

Introduction

This book is not a parenting manual, it's a book to nurture and guide you through the life-changing journey of parenthood. Book will support you through the intensity of feeling and experience that is the first year after birth. It won't tell you how to change a nappy, what colour poo your baby should have or what a great latch is. Instead, it offers you places to pause, to breathe and to feel reassured that everything you are doing is okay.

There are tools to help you understand that you have it within you to overcome the challenges such as sleepless nights, colic and feeding, and to illuminate the everyday magic of a smile, a giggle or the tug of your hair. Finding balance in everyday parenting will sustain you and give you the tools to create a strong foundation in the first year, which will make a positive difference in the years to come.

Although it may feel as if everything has led up to this moment of welcoming your new baby, there is no full stop after birth. When your baby is born everything changes overnight; suddenly this little person, who had limited movement, who was nourished and fed from within you, now has a new set of requirements you need to learn. And learn fast. From the first moment you hold your gorgeous tiny human, this little person you made, life takes on a whole new meaning.

Not only that, there are incredible changes happening in your brain that switch on your maternal, parenting, mind, influencing how you instinctively care for your baby. Forget the disempowering notion of 'baby brain' and instead see it as a positive, powerful restructuring of how your brain shifts and reorganises itself in order to nurture, protect, love and care for your baby. It doesn't matter whether you are a mother, father or parent, whether you have adopted your baby or used a surrogate mother; these brain changes will happen when you connect and bond with your baby with focused attention.

Creating a calm environment within you and around you, to allow for these physical and emotional changes to happen in their own time, can help to make your transition into parenthood, and for the first year, as gentle as possible. There are also tools and visualisations in this book that will help with the healing that comes after birth, helping you to heal and grow from the inside out, from the early weeks of the fourth trimester through to the time when you go back to work.

In the first year, becoming a mother and a parent can be an incredibly joyful experience, but it can also be difficult and confusing. Simple, adaptable psychological tools can help you to calmly, confidently and comfortably grow into the mother and parent that you are going to be. Mindfulness and hypnosis skills can be learned quickly and are remarkably effective in helping you to connect with the intense experience of becoming a parent without it becoming overwhelming.

I faced many common challenges as a new mother. The day after my first son's birth I was sent home achy, sore, vulnerable, tired, getting to grips with breastfeeding, getting to know my son. I wanted to be the perfect mother for the little baby curled in my arms. I was scared that I wouldn't, and couldn't, be what he needed. What I didn't know then was that perfect doesn't exist. Instead, a 'good-enough' mother is the perfect mother and there are so many ways you can be a good-enough mother.

With both my boys, sometimes I was slow to pick up, wished I could be alone, put nappies on back to front, and felt guilty that I didn't spend enough time focused on them. Did I listen to them enough? Did I respond quickly enough? Not always. My boys are older now, and I realise now that my good-enough was enough. Yours will be too.

I learned many of these techniques during my second pregnancy, carrying them through to the postnatal period, when I nurtured and nourished myself by adapting and using them to help with the challenges I had faced during the first year. I wanted to make motherhood as easy on myself, my husband and my children as it could be. Second time around was completely different to my first experience; using these techniques I found it easier, even with two children under the age of 18 months.

Self-hypnosis techniques provided comfort and calm when I needed permission to let go, and motivation and drive when I needed to get on with things that I'd done a hundred times already that week.

Mindfulness also became a close friend on my parenting journey. Mindfulness was introduced to me after I had my children and I attended a retreat with the Buddhist teacher and monk, Thich Nhat Hanh. It was a transformative experience. As a parent I adapted aspects of what I learned, making it simple and easy to integrate into our busy lives. I didn't have time to do much so I had to learn to use the time I had to introduce these skills into my life in ways that made a difference to my wellbeing. That's how I've approached the techniques in this book: they are simple, but they work because they are easy to integrate into your life.

It's not just about how you do things, it's also about who you are becoming. Amidst all the nappies, feeding and exhaustion is the person you are, and the mother you are becoming. Connecting with that person, and with the emerging mother in you, needs time, reflection, love and support. Even though a paucity of time as a new parent makes this seem impossible, it *is* possible. A slight shifting of the lens on who you are, and what you are capable of, makes everything suddenly seem different and more things seem possible than before. Meeting your own needs is as important as meeting your baby's needs, and this book explores some simple and meaningful ways to do this.

My first book, *Mindful Hypnobirthing*, prepared for birth with mindfulness, hypnosis and practical techniques – this book picks up where that left off. Between these pages you will find hypnosis and mindfulness exercises, accompanied by downloadable tracks, that will help you to ride all the ups and downs of the first year after your baby is born.

When people say to you, 'It just gets harder', well, it's not true. It does get easier; it's just different at every stage. Although sometimes it may not feel that way, I can guarantee that you will get a night's sleep again and you will drink a hot cup of tea again! One day, perhaps even after you have finished this book, you will realise that being a mother was a part of you that is evolving and growing, just as other parts of your personality have evolved and grown all through your life, coming together to make you the perfectly unique mother for your baby.

How to Use the Book

The book follows the first year after birth and should initially be read cover-to-cover – this way you can familiarise yourself with the exercises and understand what is where in the book. However, I understand that, as a new parent, your time may be limited, so all the chapters can be dipped into as and when you need them.

Make the book your own; scribble your thoughts on these pages, adding your own ideas as they arise. Each chapter should only take a short time to read; if you were to set 15 to 20 minutes aside for each chapter it would be enough. I've deliberately made chapters like 'Tough Days' shorter to meet your needs – you can dip in and connect with a technique in minutes.

Affirmations are scattered throughout the book; you can say them in your head and out loud. They are moments to pause and to feel more connected to the meaning behind the chapter. Seeds of calm and confidence, they will take root and blossom in you as you go through the book. Some of the affirmations are also designed to be traced with a pencil. When you write over them, the action of writing helps you take ownership of that statement; it's a very powerful form of change. You can also write them out and stick them up around your home. We go into more detail on how to write your own affirmations and why they are important in Chapter 2.

After Chapter 2, you will notice the instruction **PRESS PAUSE** throughout the book. They may appear to be quite random, but they help you to stop where you are and consciously tune into your breathing and to have a mindful moment. In those moments, use your **Calm Breath** (see page 49) to connect with a deep, belly breath.

YOU WILL NEED:

To make the most of the exercises in the book, here are a few things you will need.

- A notebook or a journal to write notes in.
- A small jar for the gratitude practice.
- Sticky notes for some of the exercises in the book.
- A device to download the tracks onto.

Part One: It's Not Just Breathing: Tools for Confidence and Calm

You'll learn why mindfulness and hypnosis are the perfect companions in your first year of parenting and what a difference they can make, not just in your day-to-day life, but in your thoughts and feelings around becoming a mother. We'll explore acceptance, gratitude, aspects of hypnosis and the foundation breathing techniques. These aspects of mindfulness and hypnosis are woven throughout the book and are tailored for specific experiences in the first year. Understanding why these tools work and how to use them is a vital part of this book.

Part Two: Welcoming your Baby

This section is for the early weeks of getting to know your baby, learning why it's important to slow down and connect with baby, while also allowing yourself and your partner time to adjust to the changes. The techniques are simple tools that help you let go of expectation and adapt to this life-altering experience. You'll learn ways to enhance bonding and connection, as well as how to create a space at home, and in your heart, for the ups and downs that new mothers and parents experience.

Part Three: Caring for You, Caring for your Baby

As you leave your nest the world looks very different with a baby. This section equips you with tools that you can integrate into your busy life as a new parent. It covers topics that you may experience in the first 12 weeks (your fourth trimester), but which may resurface throughout the first year. These may be exhaustion, feeding and finding support but also the tough days that you feel will never end. You'll find that you can dip in and out of these chapters and will put these to good use throughout the year; these are the techniques you will come back to time and time again. You may want to put markers in the pages that you find work really well for you.

Part Four: Embracing the mother in you

Becoming a mother is a big change; thoughts and feelings about yourself and your identity are in flux. As mothers we set very high expectations for ourselves, when really we need to be kinder and gentler. In this part of the book there are tools to help you connect with your instincts. You can find ways to connect with who you are, while not losing sight of what is important to you. Though it can be hard becoming a mother, it doesn't mean you should be hard on yourself. This part of the book explores the burdens we place on ourselves as mothers, encouraging forgiveness and inward-facing kindness.

Online supporting material

There are a number of free tracks to download at www.
penguin.co.uk/mindfulmamma. Download these so you can
listen to them when you wish. Whenever there is an audio
track to go with an exercise you will see this symbol 🎧.

There are tracks to increase confidence and calm; they
can be listened to at any time that you choose. I'd advise listening to at least one of these a day. You can listen to them
when feeding, dropping off to sleep and so on. We will come
back to the tracks throughout the book. Do not listen to
them while driving.

- Confident Mamma (20 mins)
- Affirmations (one from each chapter) (5 mins)
- Calm Breath (5 mins)

These tracks are specific to a chapter or an experience and
can be used as and when you like:

- Dynamic Sleep
- Forgiveness and Letting Go
- Calmer Crying
- Honouring your Journey

Please note: if you have problems accessing any of the
tracks, please contact Penguin Random House.

Mindful Mamma Checklist

You can print it out (see page 9) and put it somewhere you
can see it as a reminder, or you can write your own out on
sticky notes around the house.

Mindful Mamma Checklist

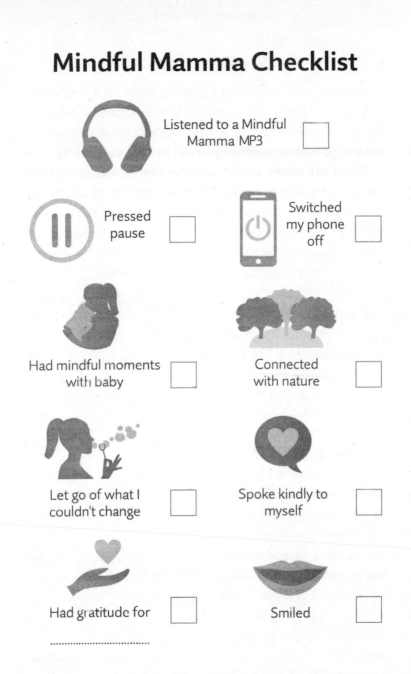

Listened to a Mindful Mamma MP3 ☐

Pressed pause ☐

Switched my phone off ☐

Had mindful moments with baby ☐

Connected with nature ☐

Let go of what I couldn't change ☐

Spoke kindly to myself ☐

Had gratitude for ☐
....

Smiled ☐

List of exercises by page

This list of exercises will help you refer back to exercises you love, quickly and easily. You may find the Breathe-Baby-Connect (see page 97) helpful when your baby is in that fragile state of between sleep. Or you may find that the Bubble of Confidence and Calm (see page 138) is great if you are in situations that make you feel uncomfortable. All the techniques can be used any time, anywhere. They are designed to create calm space within and around you and to give you the confidence you need to give you, your baby and your partner the best start in your life together.

Contacting the author

Get in contact! Writing makes me happy as I love to share these tools and hear how you put them to use. If you are running an event or workshop, why not ask me to come and share some tips and techniques? I also run a project called #specialplaces that you can join in with. You can find further resources at mindfulmamma.co.uk or sophiefletcher.co.uk or at Youtube: Mindful Mamma & Mindful Hypnobirthing.

You can join me and the Mindful Mamma community on Facebook at Mindful Mamma, The First Year, or on Instagram @sophiefletcher_author where you can find additional techniques, support and guidance.

See you there!

Sophie

part one

It's Not Just Breathing: Tools for Confidence and Calm

1

Mindfulness and Hypnosis for Self-care

Wellbeing of mind is like a mountain lake without ripples. When the lake has no ripples, everything in the lake can be seen. When the water is all churned up, nothing can be seen.

Pema Chödrön

When I first trained as a clinical hypnotherapist, it blew me away. It's a therapy that makes things happen. It can make you feel stronger, motivated and more confident in any situation that you choose. Seeing people use the tools I teach to reach their goals and improve their wellbeing has shown me that the mind is powerful and can be your best friend.

My work started to broaden in 2008 after I attended my first mindfulness retreat with Thich Nhat Hanh (known by his followers as Thay), a Buddhist monk. Not just content with a day's introduction on my own, I threw myself in and took the boys, who were two and three years old at the time. The retreat was a silent retreat for families. Yes, you read that correctly, a two-year-old and a three-year-old on a week-long silent retreat. Was I mad?

It seems not. In that week, I learned more about compassion, kindness, patience, love, gratitude, anger, frustration and letting go than I could have ever imagined possible in such a short space of time. After a mindful walk with the children, my mother and Thay, I just sat down and sobbed. I couldn't stop and I didn't care. It was as if all the guilt, doubt, worry, stress and exhaustion that I had battled in those last three years just melted away. None of it mattered. It was one of the few times in those three years that I felt complete peace as a new parent, and in that peace I remember just looking at my children and feeling the most intense joy.

His easy-to-adopt approach to mindfulness had a profound effect on me, and it still does. He taught me that mindfulness does not have to be complicated – its power sits in its simplicity. You can choose to go deeper into what is known as 'practice' if you wish and explore meditation and mindfulness in all its forms, but mindfulness is there for everyone, including you. Even if you just have a few minutes a day, you can choose to access that space where you can be still, a place of peace.

Using a mix of hypnosis and mindfulness has given me a wide range of tools I can draw on, and I have used them for virtually everything that parenting has thrown at me. Best of all, my children are benefiting too.

What is mindfulness?

Thich Nhat Hanh describes mindfulness as 'an energy that brings awareness to the present moment'. However, this isn't a rushing-around type of energy; it's an energy to be in 'intentional stillness', even if just for 10 seconds. Often, as we get on with our busy lives, we do not see what is right there in that moment, or if it is too painful and upsetting, we may push it away, avoiding it. With mindfulness, you can find stillness within you, and the capacity to look deeply, accepting whatever arises and exists in that moment.

Learning mindfulness can be a foundation for compassionate and loving parenting. However busy your life is, you can be in the moment – you may find it no extra effort to go there, as it's where you are already.

Stop now, breathe deeply. Notice the space in which you are sitting or lying. Notice your body, where it is sitting or lying. You may be holding the book in your hand, you may be listening to audio. Take another deep breath in, then breathe out and pause, and just for a moment allow yourself to be. Nowhere else, but right here now.

When you become a parent, many unexpected feelings may arise. It may be challenging to notice those feelings and be reminded of the tools that can help in the moments you need them most. There are days when I really have to dig deep and accept that I won't get anything done. There are days when I'm not the swan, looking serene with legs paddling madly under the surface, because I look as frazzled as I feel. The only thing left to do is accept it and bring it back to basics. Taking each moment, one breath at a time.

When you remind yourself to take a breath and slow down, just doing one task slowly and with deep intent, it will make you feel better. The first time you may not notice the difference, but the more you do it the more easily you will find that space within and around you. The effect of these small moments is cumulative; it's like training a muscle.

Even changing your baby's nappy can be an opportunity for mindfulness. However slowly you are doing it, see if you can do it more slowly.

'While I am changing my baby's nappy, I am putting all my focus on my baby. I am present with my baby, I am giving tender, gentle loving care in this moment and with each wipe I am lovingly caring for my baby. As I am putting my baby's nappy on, I am cleaning and caring for my baby. As I am putting the nappy in the bin, I am creating a clean environment for my baby.'

If your baby is crying and fretful, connect with your breathing, grounding yourself with your breath. Try this now: as you breathe in, say 'breathing in' in your mind, and as you breathe out, say 'breathing out'. Do it once at your normal pace, and then do it again slower, and then do it a third time, doing it slower still.

'Breathing in and breathing out.'

'As I stroke my baby's back I am stroking their discomfort away, as I am rocking my baby, I am rocking myself, as I am wiping my baby's tears away, I am wiping away my worry, as I am humming soothingly for my baby, I am soothing myself.'

You can use these many times during the day, with simple tasks that may have been done mindlessly before. Next time you do something you have done hundreds of times before, connect with the task in hand – take the actions slowly, carefully, one at a time. With mindful awareness you start to create a deep capacity within you, to accept and calmly address the things that arise on your parenting journey.

The benefits of mindfulness

Mindfulness can help you slow down day-to-day, rather than rushing around. Regular practice can also be part of your lifestyle medicine, as it can:

- create positive changes in the brain
- improve self-regulation
- improve memory

- reduce stress
- help with illness
- help with fatigue

What is hypnosis?

The type of hypnosis that many people are familiar with is the impression of controlling hypnotists with spiral eyes, top hats and swinging watches. Thankfully that image is starting to change now, but still the assumption persists that a hypnotherapist can make you do anything they want you to. In fact, the opposite is true. A hypnotherapist is more of a guide, helping you find a way to change a habit, behaviour or feeling.

The most important tool in a hypnotherapist's box is language, and the power of suggestion. Professor of Psychology Irving Kirsch claims, 'there is no hypnosis, only suggestion'. This can be demonstrated through the power of placebo; if we are given a drug and told it is going to help with back pain, or depression or many other things, it can be very effective.

Remarkably, studies show that even if we are told we are receiving a placebo it can still create a significant change in the experience of pain, or mental wellbeing. There are studies where a placebo spray was shown to help heal a 'broken' heart. Your thoughts can change your physical experience purely through suggestion or language. This can be words spoken to you by others, or words you speak to yourself.

EXERCISE 1: THE BODY–MIND CONNECTION

This exercise can help you to understand how your thoughts can activate real sensations in your body. This one is particularly powerful because most people have a strong emotional response to lice. If you were afraid of spiders and did this exercise with spiders instead of lice, it would evoke an even stronger response. As I'm writing this now, just the suggestion of lice is triggering the need to scratch!

You can do this exercise by reading it to yourself quietly, or reading it to your partner, or your partner or friend can read it to you. Maybe try it with different people and see if they respond differently.

Just for a moment, just where you are, notice your head, and bring head lice into your mind; you know, those tiny little creatures that jump from head to head, quickly and stealthily. Think of one that has managed to leap onto your head, imagine it now laying eggs and those tiny lice, scuttling around your hair, nesting, moving. It may even feel as if your hair is moving, or your scalp is itching as you imagine them moving around. Perhaps you feel itchy already, not just on your scalp but other areas of your body, behind your ears or the top of your arms; perhaps you can picture one in your mind, those little legs nesting in your hair.

The suggestion of lice can create a physical sensation. If you can create a sensation, you can *change* a sensation too. Knowing that your mind has the power to do that can be one of the first steps on your path to harnessing its capacity for change. All change is interesting; all change shows us that we can make physical adjustments with our thoughts. Imagine how powerful this could be for you on a day-to-day basis. Even though suggestion on its own is powerful, as Professor Kirsch explains, being in hypnosis can have a role to play in engaging with change more deeply too.

Studies have now started to use brain imaging to understand what is happening when people are in hypnosis. A study at Stamford University in 2016 shows how brain activity changes. These changes are consistent with feedback I have from people who undergo hypnosis: they often experience sensory changes; someone may feel heavier or lighter, or they may feel like they are drifting. As the brain changes under hypnosis, it strengthens the brain – body connection in a way that helps the brain process and control what's going on in the body. A suggestion to feel light may actually make you feel lighter. This is why is can be so effective for pain-management.

How does hypnosis feel? It feels amazing. It's like not quite being awake or not quite being asleep. It may feel as if you are sleeping and that's okay. What you are doing is resting in that space while your mind rejigs itself, to align its actions with the changes you want to make. You'll come out of hypnosis very easily if you need to, even during listening to a track. Remember, you are the one who is in control and your mind is always on alert at a deep level. If you are listening and your baby wakes up, you will wake up too. If you have headphones on it will be harder to hear your baby, so if you do need to be 'on call' it is better to listen through speakers.

> ✆ You can download the **Confident Mamma** track and affirmations that can be listened to on a regular basis, either with the book or on their own. This hypnosis track is great for boosting general confidence and helping to relax your body and mind. You can listen to this when you are dropping off to sleep, during the day, just once a week, or five days a week; it's up to you!

The changes that you experience with hypnosis can be very subtle; my clients often say: 'I feel so much calmer, but I can't quite put my finger on why.' The results of hypnotherapy may not be felt immediately, but there may be a growing sense of adjustment during the days and weeks following therapy; a lightness of feeling.

Hypnosis is very specific – it's about being focused on *change*, and this is often why it's called 'solutions-focused', or 'goal-driven'. You decide how you want to make a habit, behaviour or feeling different and better, then you listen to hypnosis tracks or visualisations that focus on this.

People usually think of hypnosis as 'going into a trance', but another powerful aspect of my practice is 'reframing'. This is presenting something in a different way, to help you see and experience something from other perspectives. It can be done without hypnosis but it is especially powerful when done in hypnosis, as it bypasses your inner critic. When you change your perspective, you create the potential to change your experience. When I wrote my first book, I was told 'there weren't as many hypnosis techniques in it as I expected but I felt my confidence grow as I read it.' The true power of hypnosis, and the skill of a hypnotherapist, is about giving you the support, vision and meaning to make a difference yourself – deeply, unconsciously and independently.

How are mindfulness and hypnosis different?

Both can help you at different times throughout your journey as a parent. Often people say they really don't understand the difference as they feel very similar. Sometimes they can feel similar. However, they are different!

If you are experienced in meditation and mindfulness, you can bring your existing knowledge to the exercises in this book. For the purposes of this book mindfulness can be described as mind maintenance, attitudes and practical techniques to stay attentive to what is happening in the moment. Mindfulness is something that you can cultivate for the long term; it's a foundation for your wellbeing as a parent and will serve you well as your baby grows into a toddler, tween, teenager and adult.

Hypnosis can be seen as a goal orientated practice: for example, you may want to turn your milk flow up or down, you may want to change a feeling or sensation in your body, or you may wish to set yourself some targets that you want to work towards.

When you enter into hypnosis or a state of mindfulness, you create a stronger link between the insula (an instinctive part of your brain) and the pre-frontal cortex (the part of your brain that regulates your responses). You also decrease activity in the part of your brain that is the communications centre, the part where your internal narrator lives. Sometimes people say to me that they find it difficult to switch off the chatter at first, but the more you practise the techniques in the book the easier this will be.

Your internal narrator

Your internal narrator is the part of your brain that is incessantly talking to you; it's the voice that can quieten down during hypnosis and mindfulness – it's often known as self-talk. Your brain will chatter with you throughout the day. The messages that you receive may be positive, negative or neutral. Learning to understand this self-talk and recognise it for what it is will help you to work with it so that it benefits you. When you approach self-talk in this way it can help you feel more positive, confident and capable, especially as you are learning to become a mother. Would you say to your best friend, or to your child, the things you say to yourself?

Paying attention to these messages can help to understand and get to know the mother in you; it can help you know that you are able to learn, change and grow into this new part of your identity.

EXERCISE 2: IS IT HELPFUL, IS IT TRUE?

This exercise will help you to notice and really hear and connect in a positive way with your internal narrator. It will help you to identify the narrative that is playing in your head – always remember that your narrator is *you*, and that you have the power to change the messages if they are unhelpful. Often the narrator's voice drowns out the present moment by ruminating on the past or projecting into the future.

Consider some of the messages that you receive from your internal narrator, then ask yourself:

- Is it helpful?
- Is it true?

Now recall a time and place when you were completely present. Close your eyes and recall the detail. Connect with your senses and name three things you notice about being in that moment. (If you can't find three, just find one.)

Notice how when you focus your mind, it silences your narrator and their story of maybes, might-bes and might-have-beens. Doesn't that feel calmer?

By taking just small steps to adjust the lens on your life, learning to see each detail, you will be able to quieten the internal narrator down. This helps you to be kind to yourself and to really connect with your baby and with the changes within you, at a pace that feels right and comfortable for you.

When you practise mindfulness, listen to the guided audio or use the hypnosis techniques in this book regularly; it's like exercising a muscle. The more you do it, the stronger the connection becomes between the areas of your brain that help with self-regulation. This can help you find a place of calm, even in moments that may have otherwise caused stress, in a way that feels automatic.

How mindfulness and hypnosis help you as a new parent

When you become a parent, you may find it is much how you expected, or it may be very different. The journey you are on is *your* journey, and walking that path with an open heart and with acceptance of where that path will take you can be one of the most profound lessons in life. Parenting can give you so much, but it can also challenge you to look deeply within, at who you are and how you behave. Your thoughts, feelings and actions may surprise you, they may upset you, and they may bring you joy.

This path can sometimes be uncomfortable and mindfulness can teach you to sit with those feelings, accepting them as they are without fighting or avoiding them. Hypnosis can help motivate yourself to set goals and to use practical techniques, such as visualisation, to improve your wellbeing. In my journey as a parent, I have been angry, frustrated, weary and fearful but I have also felt happiness and love beyond anything I ever felt before. When I became a parent, all of these feelings seemed more exaggerated than ever. I also felt powerless to control them sometimes, until I learned that it wasn't about control; it was about accepting that those feelings were *there*. I made friends with them; I might not always like them, but now I say hello and I let them float on by instead of pushing them down.

Mindfulness helps you to see the development of your baby; the tiny, everyday things such as the twitch of your baby's mouth as they fall into sleep, developing into a full-blown smile two days later and into a giggle a few weeks after that. As you notice the moments, both happy and sad, you see *all* of parenting, and can learn how to embrace the inevitable ups and downs with awareness and understanding of the big picture.

Many of the exercises throughout the book that can help you to see things in a different and better way are grounded in hypnotherapy. They can help you to change your perspective and put practical steps in place to make things happen. Many of these exercises are designed to fit seamlessly with the audio and will encourage you to adjust and make changes that will benefit your wellbeing.

There is no better time to begin simple mindfulness exercises and hypnosis techniques than in the early days of parenting. Everything appears to slow down as you emerge from your pregnancy with a baby, and all the changes that come with that, whether they are emotional or physical. Mindfulness can help you adjust and adapt to being a parent, and can help you face the challenges those changes may throw at you, as well as the moments of joy. Slowing down implies you will have all this time to do all of this, but it's a different type of slowness – somehow baby takes up most of that space and it can be hard to see time for your own self-care.

I know it felt like that with my two; it's so fresh in my memory, and sometimes it felt as if I was going nowhere fast. But often expectation of what I 'should' have been doing created a conflict, and I fought that slowness, when instead I needed to lean into the slowness.

You may be catapulted from a busy life, you may have worked up to the last minute to capture as much maternity leave as possible, unprepared for the transition of becoming a parent.

For you this time may offer a huge opportunity to stop and slow down, to connect with your baby and to use this experience as a mindfulness process. It can be a release from goals, deadlines and timetables. When you are really with your baby you can *see* your baby; you commit each wrinkle of your baby's foot, your baby's smile to memory. To go slow can be a gift.

Throughout the book you are going to learn more about how to do this, even when it may be really challenging to find stillness within you; there will be tracks and simple tools to help you. You are not alone, you are part of a growing community of Mindful Mammas.

How mindfulness and hypnosis will help your baby

I don't have to tell you; I'm sure that you are already aware that babies are absolutely present in each moment. They do not need to learn how to be mindful. They let you know when they are hungry, when their nappy is dirty, when they can't sleep and they need comfort. What they do feel is your tension, stress, worry and 'mindlessness'. These are perfectly normal states of being human, and babies will also have to learn about them, but how you respond to them will create the blueprint for how they will respond. It doesn't have to be perfect, it just needs to be good enough.

When you soften and lean into the moment, using mindfulness to connect with your breath, you create a shift in two systems in your body: the sympathetic nervous system (we know this as 'fight, flight or freeze'), and your para-sympathetic nervous system – your soothing system.

Your fight, flight or freeze system is your stress response, it's a heightened state of alert. If it senses a threat, its goal is to get you out of where you are, or for you to play dead, which you may be more familiar with as fainting. A stress response increases your breathing rate and heart rate and creates tension in your body as you get ready to fight or sprint away.

Your soothing system, on the other hand, is a natural resting state; it slows your breathing down, slows your heart rate down, and the muscles in your body soften. As a human being you are only meant to be in a heightened state of alert in short bursts. These short bursts are nature's way of helping you get out of a threatening situation. However, stress is epidemic in our society and many people are in a heightened state of alert more often, and longer, than they should be.

Your baby can feel the difference. It can be really helpful to know an activity that can engage your soothing system, such as using a lengthening breath. The **Calm Breath**, on page 49, slows your breathing down, then your heart rate, followed by the softening of the muscles in your body. I will remind you to use this simple breath throughout the book in **PRESS PAUSE**.

Try this exercise to see how it feels to be held by someone who is tense and then relaxed:

EXERCISE 3: A HUG FROM A CALM HEART

Stand opposite a friend or a partner. Start with the person opposite you tensing up, really tensing up in their body, shoulders and jaw, and scrunching their fists up as tight as they can. Now hug that person while they are feeling so tense. Then stand back and ask them to shake it out, take a few deep breaths and relax, right into their hands and shoulders. Now hug them again. How different is that? Many of the exercises in this book are about reducing tension, so you will be a lot softer to hug!

Feeling tense?

There will be moments when you feel tense while holding your baby, and that's normal. You just need to notice it and take steps to adjust it when you can.

Your baby isn't looking for a perfect parent; your baby wants a parent who responds to them, cares for them and makes them feel loved and safe in a world that is completely new and unexplored. It's normal to be tired, to get cross, to cry, to not have time to do all the household jobs or skip the bedtime routine as you just couldn't summon up the energy.

Responding to your baby's needs mindfully will help your baby. They are looking for cues and guidance on how to respond to life's up and downs from you. Everything is a wonder to them – each new sensation, touch, sound and smell is laying down a map in their brain that will help them navigate the world around them. As early as their first month, babies can start to make expressions, even trying to mimic you. Practising mindfulness allows you to slow to baby's pace during this important time of their development. When you slow down, and connect deeply with what they truly need, you are allowing the gentle pathways of their map to imprint into the folds of their brain.

Your baby is watching you, learning from you, and you are teaching them to use tools of resilience for life without even thinking about it. How wonderful a gift to receive from your mother!

The importance of self-care

There is so much on the news and online about self-care; what does it really mean and why is it so important? Self-care is taking steps to do what you can to ensure *your* emotional and physical wellbeing. If you have not cared for yourself in the most basic of ways, it is hard for you to care for anyone else. Self-care is not 'selfish' – taking care of yourself means that you can take care of your baby.

Self-care for a new parent can be practical things like washing, going to the loo, eating well. You are not alone if you find you haven't washed your hair for a few days, or are eating the same foods every day! Ensuring that you have seen to the most basic aspects of hygiene and nourishment is especially important for new mothers like you, who have to care for their physical changes as well as emotional ones. In many parts of the world, the first 40 days (or the 'fourth trimester') is a time supported by family and friends, in which a new mother can be nurtured, so she can nurture baby. In the book we'll explore postnatal care and encourage you to prepare to have plans and people in place that make it easier for you to find those moments for essential self-care.

Mindfulness and hypnosis are about meeting your basic psychological needs and are an important part of any self-care routine postnatally. Self-care, as a part of your motherhood journey, should explore some of the emotional and psychological aspects of wellbeing. This includes maintaining aspects of your life that are familiar and create a sense of joy. The things that make you, you. It can be very difficult to find time for self-care as a new parent as it will often feel as if baby's needs come first, and they do most of the time. Someone always needs to be meeting the needs of your baby, and even when they are sleeping it will feel that there are things to do. In the very early days, often your baby's needs and yours can be met at the same time. We will go into examples of this in the book.

On the self-care front, I'm not afraid to say to my husband when he gets in from work that I need to take some time out after a day at home with both of my girls. Normally this means I take myself up to my bedroom with a book or some trashy magazines and a big bar of chocolate. The peace and quiet, and being able to focus on my needs, feels like heaven, and recharges my batteries a bit so I can then plough on until bedtime. Normally just 30–45 minutes is all I need to feel the benefits of this.

Jemma, mother of two children

When mothers say 'I can't even go to the loo on my own,' they are really saying 'I can't get any time alone.' However, there are moments of time that you *can* find, moments that allow you to find that space within; it doesn't need to be behind the loo door, and you don't need to be alone to do it. Sometimes self-care is changing your perspective about what self-care is, how it needs to be done, and where it needs to be done.

As baby grows, and you emerge from the first few months, it is time to start to think creatively about when you can set aside time to care for yourself. Rather than just moments, you may find it easier to create pockets of time to connect with yourself, and your needs. This way you can find balance within you.

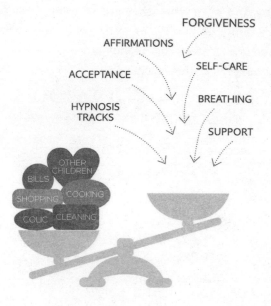

Summary

Being mindful is connecting deeply with the present moment through observation, and *acceptance* of a feeling or experience. Hypnosis is about taking steps to *change* a feeling, habit or behaviour by using techniques to change what your experience is. You may find that one works for you better than the other in different situations. With both, the more you practise the easier it gets. Neither take much time but they can both improve the quality of the time you have. In the next chapter we'll explore a range of different techniques that you can take forward into practice during the first year and beyond.

2

Mastering the Tools

*You become what you practise, so practise what
you want to become.*

At times it may feel as if it's impossible to find time to do
anything else when your life is full of your baby's needs.
Your needs are important too; you already know that, don't
you? But it can be tough to even think about your needs, let
alone meet them. The exercises in this book can be simple
additions to your routine, and a reminder of when the tools
can help the most. They are not about finding *more* time
but using the time you have to connect with the emerging
mother in you, with your baby and the day-to-day experiences of parenting.

Even if you haven't used hypnosis or mindfulness before
you will find these techniques easy to pick up and to use.
When you use them often you will find that you learn to
love them as many parents have done before you. You may
find that they automatically spill over into other areas of
your life and using them will become habitual. Many
parents say that using the techniques helped them to
adjust to their baby's pace – as if there is more space inside
them, in which to respond to their and their baby's needs.
It's a little bit like magic, and we could all use a little magic
in our lives.

You can use gentle hypnosis exercises when you are feeding baby, when you are walking, when you are falling asleep. Yes, this will happen, and you'll learn how to maximise the sleep you have for your wellbeing!

If something doesn't work, don't worry! Rest assured that you, like most people, will gravitate towards the exercises you prefer; you don't have to like doing them all. Keep it simple and as regular as you can, even if the only time you have is when you are boiling a kettle, changing a nappy, while feeding, rocking, or walking to the shops.

What to know before you get started

There are several things to think about before you read this section:

1. The book will give you quick fixes for challenges in the first year, but it is also about establishing habits that will sustain you and help you throughout all the years of parenting to come.
2. In these pages you will find your own private space for reflection. These moments will help you to connect with the aspects of yourself that are adjusting to be a parent. It gives you the opportunity to learn about your response to the world around you, lovingly and without judgement.
3. Once you reach the end of the first year you can look back and see how much you have learned, and how far you have come. You will also be able to reflect on the first year, taking joy in the memory of little things that may otherwise have been forgotten – not just the big milestones, but quirky, personal moments that matter to you and that are unique to you and your family.

Acceptance

Knowing others is intelligence, knowing
yourself is true wisdom.

Lao Tzu

Acceptance is one of the most important aspects of mindful parenting and can be a real companion during the toughest times of being a parent.

When an experience, or a feeling, is intense and over-whelming, sometimes the instinct is to change something, or to avoid it, and this may be especially true of parenting. What if the easiest option is just to accept how it is in that moment?

Imagine feelings like an energy; some are more powerful than others, but they are all just energy passing through. Acceptance is a way of opening up to this energy. It can take courage to lean into a feeling and to go deeply into what you are feeling. By leaning into the discomfort and seeing it for what it is you release the emotional charge. Though hard at first, it becomes liberating and you'll experience a lightness of being.

What you may believe to be shortcomings or failures can be seen and learned from, rather than be buried only to resurface again at a later date. When you see them and accept them for what they are in that moment, you become aware of your own vulnerability and you become stronger and more resilient for it.

Allowing yourself to be open to learning about every part of you, the dark as well as the light, with forgiveness and kindness, is how you become a self-aware parent.

But what does acceptance actually *mean* and why is it so important for you on your parenting journey?

1. **Acceptance is about opening up to all of your experiences**

   It may be very easy to accept feelings of happiness, joy and excitement, but much harder to accept feelings that aren't so positive, and which are more challenging. This is especially true of times when there are powerful transitions and changes, such as parenting. A feeling does not go away because you deny it; on the contrary – it hangs around longer! By accepting it, and naming it, it is easier to let go and to move on.

2. **Acceptance is action not inaction**

   If you were passive you would avoid those difficult feelings. Acceptance is bearing witness to those feelings, however uncomfortable, acknowledging them and then letting them go. When you choose acceptance, you are choosing to be an active participant in how you relate to and respond to that feeling in the moment. Acceptance is a practice that you cultivate. It takes patience. Those moments when you act impulsively and are remorseful? Those are the moments when you will learn to go deeper.

   Compare the two reactions to this situation:

   'My baby is crying. I am so frustrated that I can't soothe him. I feel overwhelmed, I want to walk away. Why won't he stop crying? What am I doing wrong?'

   'My baby is crying, I am feeling turmoil and frustration that I can't soothe him. Breathing in I feel calm, breathing out, I let go.'

   If you find yourself in this situation or in a situation with overwhelming feelings, focus on the feeling and notice where it is in your body. Take a deep breath and go deeper into that feeling; notice where it is. Allow yourself to be present as you notice the feeling. As you do this, the overwhelm will subside. Then use your **Calm Breath** (see page 49).

An emotion or an experience can be an opportunity for you to learn about yourself; it doesn't have to be a source of conflict and distress. Seeing your emotion as it *is* is a powerful step towards acceptance and letting go.

Gratitude

Do you practise gratitude? Do you look at where you are and what you are doing with thanks and appreciation? Studies show that a regular gratitude practice can help reduce stress at times in your life when there are big transitions. Gratitude can change how you feel, reducing the risk of depression or anxiety, increasing your satisfaction with life. When you practise gratitude, life can take on a whole new meaning.

It's usual for people to only notice and express gratitude for the big things, things that deviate from everyday life. I'd like you to think about some of the more ordinary things. Think about when you have to do things you really don't want to do: do you say 'I have to have a shower', 'I have to change his nappy' or 'I have to cook dinner'?

Pause for a moment and think about changing your language around these moments. Instead of making it seem like something that you haven't chosen to do, make it something that you have an *opportunity* to do. Instead of using 'have to', use 'get'.

'I get to have a shower.'

'I get to change his nappy.'

'I get to cook dinner.'

Try it with a few other phrases to see how different this feels. It could be gratitude for the milk you were able to feed your baby, or the clothes that you can to dress him in. This is how you can approach a task with gratitude. It reminds you that even the little, everyday things can be a gift.

A gratitude practice can shine a spotlight on those small, special moments that get lost between the big moments. Baby books and journals are often focused on first smile, first steps, first food and first words. What about all the moments in between? The moment you caught your child's eye in the rear-view mirror and she beamed at you. The moment when they threw their carrot mash on the floor for the 20th time and you accepted it and just laughed with them. Just a feeling of love, of joy, or a simple, 'I am glad that you are here.'

EXERCISE 4: MAKING GRATITUDE EASY

For this exercise you need a shoebox or a large jar, whatever you have to hand. You also need a block of sticky notelets.

Every day, write down something that you are grateful for, whether it's a look, a feeling, or simply that you have warm water to bathe your baby in at night. What brought a smile to your face, or made you feel a surge of happiness? Did something make your heart sing? Put it in your gratitude box. If you use a notes app on your phone to write, take a moment to write them up by hand when you can; it does make a difference to go through the physical process of writing.

Remember, this isn't just a nice thing to do; it has real benefits to your wellbeing, and it is one of the quickest and easiest adjustments that you can make to become a calm and confident mother.

At the end of the book we are going to come back to this exercise, and you'll learn how those moments can help you, not just for the first year, but beyond.

Affirmations (positive statements)

Affirmations are positive statements that help you to stop, pause and breathe, allowing you to connect with the moment. You will find them scattered through the book, where they will relate to the theme of that chapter.

The affirmations can help you to connect with, and nurture, the calm and confident mother in you. Affirmations are proven to help adjust your beliefs at a very deep level – a purposeful affirmation like: 'when my baby cries, I take a deep breath, I soften my body and I cuddle them calmly' shifts your perspective just enough for your mind and body to recognise that, in those moments, you are choosing to respond that way. By placing a spotlight on that possibility, it brings it into awareness, and then into action. When you say an affirmation regularly, it becomes automatic and will happen without you even having to think about it.

Studies show that affirmations can help foster resilience and can help buffer you in situations that may be challenging. They can be a very useful tool for parenting.

Let's think about positive statements. Remember the internal narrator (see page 23) part of you that is always there? It's the voice that gives you a running commentary on your life. What stories does it tell, what messages do you hear? What is your spotlight shining on? Are you kind to yourself, or are the messages you hear internally things that you would not say to another person? Would you say the things to your best friend? Can you be your own best friend?

Compare the following two thoughts:

'I'm not going to make any new friends at the baby yoga class.'

'I am open to making new friends at the baby yoga class.'

The minute you open yourself up to opportunity, you are likely to take action that enables this to happen. If you don't believe that you are going to make new friends at a baby yoga class, or it makes you feel nervous, that can stop you going, which then reaffirms the belief 'I never make friends easily' or 'I find it really hard to go to new groups'. If you believe that you are going to make new friends and are open to having a positive experience it is more likely that it *will be* a positive experience.

If you find that your thoughts throw up negative statements, you can do something called 'The positivity challenge'. This can help you to see your internal narrative from a different perspective. I use this exercise in my practice when people are persistently talking themselves down. Just for today, talk yourself up!

EXERCISE 5: THE POSITIVITY CHALLENGE

See if you can do this exercise today, and then continue, one day at a time.

1. Wake up with the goal to talk yourself up.

2. Have one affirmation like, 'today is going to be a good day,' for when you wake up.

3. Each time you have a thought of self-doubt, or find you're criticising yourself, stop. Instead think: 'If I were talking to [friend's name], what would I say?'

Being positive to yourself

Instead of saying: 'It's always raining when I want to go for a walk with the baby, I am so unlucky,'

Say:

'Ah it's raining today. Great, we can jump in some puddles/ snuggle at home and have some downtime/have a friend over.'

WRITING YOUR OWN AFFIRMATIONS

Why not write your own positive affirmations? If you use words like 'try', 'should', 'might', 'see if I can', they create a 'get-out clause' for your brain. Say in your mind: 'I'm going to try to post that letter tomorrow,' and then say: 'I'm going to post that letter tomorrow.' There is a very subtle, but meaningful, difference.

It's like the quote from Yoda in *Star Wars*: 'Do or do not, there is no try.'

Equally, never use the word don't. If I say to you right now: 'Don't turn around, whatever you do, you mustn't turn around, don't do it!' what do you want to do? Turn around of course! This is because I've given the suggestion that you *could* turn around. Instead, if I said 'look ahead' you wouldn't even consider it, would you? It's not about what you *don't* want to feel or experience, but what you *do* want to feel or experience.

Have a go at writing your own positive affirmation here. If you can't do it right now, think about it and come back to it later:

....
....
....
....
....
....
....
....
....
....
....
....
....

Journaling

Writing a diary may have been something you last did as a child, but journaling, as it is otherwise known, is evidenced to help your wellbeing. Just three times a week of 15 minutes of journaling, over a twelve-week period, has been shown to reduce anxiety and increase resilience (being able to recover quickly when things are difficult). It's important to make it easy for yourself – just a few minutes a day to jot down a few things is all you need. Some days you may wish to write more, others less. If all you can manage is a sentence one day, that's enough! If you don't manage to journal three times a week and then weeks pass between entries, it doesn't matter! Just pick it up and carry on when you can.

As you read this book, you may find that thoughts pop up or feelings arise that you may not have noticed before. You may be aware of the feelings you experience in your day-to-day life; your journal will help you to pause and notice the thoughts that may sit underneath those feelings. Journaling will help you to get in touch with a deeper part of yourself, giving you the opportunity to notice, question or just observe what changes are happening as you make the transition into motherhood.

Your journal could include:

- drawings
- collage
- prose
- poetry

Writing a journal can give you a space for creative and emotional expression. It can be a powerful keepsake, especially in that first year, when it's a blur of so many different and new experiences. If you like, consider joining a journaling group, which are springing up everywhere. There is a link to the Maternal Journal project in the resources section; or you could start a group near you!

Visualisation

Visualisation is a well-used tool in hypnosis. Very often I hear people call 'guided relaxation' hypnosis, because a good hypnotic visualisation can make you feel very relaxed. It is more than this.

When you use a visualisation, the intuitive part of your brain comes alive, through the use of metaphor and subtle shifts in language. Think of your brain as multi-lingual – your *whole brain* can speak in symbols, colour and shapes, all with deeper meaning. Your conscious mind has to filter and simplify the rich language of the unconscious into the words you use every day.

Language:

An echo of the soul

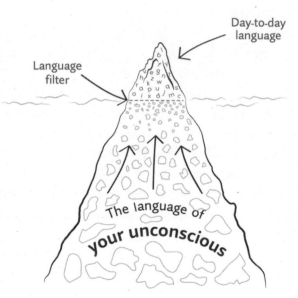

When you work with hypnotic visualisation and symbols you communicate with the deeper part of your brain. Symbols are a type of coding, and hypnosis makes good use of this. It accelerates change as it dives down into the deeper parts of your brain, allowing you to communicate with all the parts of you that need to help you make day-to-day life different and better.

In this book, and in the tracks that you can listen to alongside it, I use different types of visualisations that involve colour, symbols and images. In the book you will notice how sometimes I encourage you to give your **Calm Breath** a colour, or to imagine a feeling as a shape; this is so you can change the feeling quickly and easily without putting much conscious thought into it.

If you find it hard to 'visualise' – you are not alone. Some people are not as visual as others but connect strongly with the language of the whole brain through other senses like hearing or feeling. Even if you can't visualise you can 'imagine' something using whichever sense comes easiest to you.

Let's give it a go! Pause and imagine a beach for a moment. Think of the sand underfoot, the sound of the sea, and the feel of the wind against your skin. You can see a little boat bobbing on the waves, you can taste the salt in the air and feel the sun on your hair.

It is quite difficult to see the beach in full sensory technicolour, but you may be able to connect more with the wind or hear the sea. If you struggle to visualise, try to 'imagine' instead. Everyone I have worked with has been able to do this; if you like, try to imagine your last holiday!

USING VISUALISATION TO SET GOALS

Studies show that if you use visualisation to rehearse a goal, you are more likely to achieve that goal. Using visualisation can help you to change your responses and reactions, as well as give you an encouraging boost when you feel tired or non-committal. This is a great tool to help tackle small daily tasks when motivation is low – it can help you go and get a pint of milk when that feels insurmountable – or even longer-term goals, like what kind of parent you wish to be.

You can have:

- mini-goals for a specific task
- daily goals
- monthly goals
- long-term goals

Pause for a moment, close your eyes and imagine the colour yellow.

The part of your brain that was just activated is the same part of your brain that would be activated if you were actually looking at the colour yellow. This is important in relation to goals because it begins to fire neurons in your brain that are associated with that goal. Your brain starts to align your internal intention with external action. This can be a great tool on tough days, when you are struggling to even get out of bed.

Tip: *Use visualisation as often as you like. Remember: your goals can always change, and you can set new ones.*

EXERCISE 6: HOW TO SET A GOAL AND MAKE IT HAPPEN

You are the architect of your own mind and are capable of creating a screenplay in your mind of how you wish the day to unfold, or how you wish to parent. I love this technique because it harnesses your imagination and creativity. By creating a visualisation in your mind and then becoming a participant, you are inhabiting that experience as if it were really happening. This is the first step to making your goals a reality.

Let's start! Sit quietly somewhere. You can do this when your baby is asleep on you, when your baby is feeding, or as you are drifting off to sleep at night. You could try it when you are a passenger in a car. It's like daydreaming; just close your eyes and imagine your film unfolding with you as both the director and the lead actor. You'll notice how much calmer you feel when you are parenting in the way you want to. Here are some ideas to help you visualise your film:

- Imagine that you are creating a film of you mothering.
- Create the role. What kind of mother do you want to be?
  Close your eyes and imagine you are a calm and confident parent today. What does a calm and confident parent mean to you? Imagine stepping into the role of that mother.
- If a challenge pops up imagine yourself dealing with it.
- Use your directing skills to set up that scenario exactly how you want it to play out.
- Experience how good it feels to parent authentically, the way you want to.
- Keep that experience in your head and your heart.

Tip: *You can do this each morning for a few minutes to set yourself up for the day. Soon you may find that you feel calmer, and that you respond in the way that you want without having to think about it.*

Breathing

Breathing techniques are so effective and easy to use. Learn the simple ones in this book and they will make a difference in the moments that matter. We all know how to breathe, but your breath changes according to how you are feeling. Learning how to master this and how to change it for your wellbeing will benefit you for the rest of your life.

If you are anxious, worried or stressed, your breathing changes and your breaths become shorter; it's known as a 'state of alert'. Temporarily, this is a normal response of your stress system (your sympathetic nervous system), but being in a state of alert without a break may affect your physical and mental health.

Regularly using opportunities to breathe consciously and deeply activates your para-sympathetic nervous system (your soothing system), and can help you to let go of any stress or anxiety that may be building up. When you switch into the **Calm Breath** (see below), you will feel yourself becoming more and more relaxed. Breathing consciously may be more than just feeling calm; it can trigger calm behaviour, as researchers at Stanford University have observed. Mark Krasnow, who ran a study on this subject, called this part of the brain's function 'a pacemaker for breathing'.

Calm Breath helps you connect with yourself in that moment, because that is all there really is, the moment you are in. Bringing yourself back into the present moment helps to ground you and help you regain a foothold in what is real right now.

EXERCISE 7: YOUR CALM BREATH

If you are busy or feeling overwhelmed, using **Calm Breath** is a lovely, short and simple way of grounding yourself in the moment. Use it regularly to help you to centre yourself when you feel as if things are getting too much. When you breathe in, your heart rate increases a little, but when you breathe out it slows down. If you are anxious, you may find that you are breathing in short, shallow breaths and that you linger on the in-breath, sometimes unconsciously holding the [or] your breath, so focus on lengthening your out-breath.

As a minimum, do one of these a day. The more you repeat it, the more you will do it without even thinking. It can be for as little as 10 seconds. You can find 10 seconds, can't you?

1. Pause for a moment where you are.
2. Put one hand on your chest and one hand on your belly.
3. Close your eyes and just notice your breathing as you are. Notice the rise and fall of your hands, your breath, and notice which hand is moving more than the other.
4. If the hand on your chest is moving more than your belly, consciously switch – imagining you are blowing up a balloon in your belly. Your belly breath = calm breath. If the hand on your belly moved more, deepen that breath next time.
5. As you breathe in, say in your mind: '3 … 2 … 1 …'
6. As you breathe out, say in your mind: 'relax … relax … relax …' Lengthen the out-breath on the words 'relax' by slowing the words down in your mind.

Tip: *To master the art of a lengthening out-breath, imagine you are softly blowing a dandelion clock, and all the seeds are floating away into the wind.*

🎧 *When you listen to the **Calm Breath** audio you will notice how as you breathe out, you slow your out-breath down.*

PRESS PAUSE

Throughout the book you will see the words **PRESS PAUSE**. When you see this put your hands on your belly and your chest, and use your **Calm Breath** to connect with your breathing in that moment. Use the opportunity to check in, connect, slow down and take a breather.

If you like, write **PRESS PAUSE** on sticky notes and put them around your home as a reminder to just stop and focus on how you are breathing.

How to personalise the Calm Breath

The way you use your **Calm Breath** will be much more effective if you learn it in your own, unique way. You learn through your senses and one will be more dominant, so why don't you have a go at each of them and see which works best for you? You will find that one of these ways will relax you more quickly.

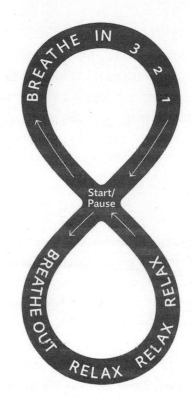

See:

Look at the image, close your eyes, and see the image in your mind. I want you to imprint this image in your mind, so that when you do **Calm Breath** you can pull it up in your mind and follow it visually wherever you are. You could also print off the image from the www.penguin.co.uk/mindfulmamma and put it up in your home so that you can see it often as a reminder.

Feel:

Look at the image. With your forefinger, trace the number '8' on your forehead in time with your breath; you could draw it on its side or upright. You could also try tracing it on the palm of your hand, or just above your navel. Follow your breath upwards as you breathe in, and then downwards as you breathe out.

Hear:

Download the **Calm Breath** track (see page 49). Choose a moment when your baby is sleeping or with someone else, so you can relax.

HOW MUCH TIME DO YOU HAVE?

I don't know how much time you have, but I am sure, like most new parents, you feel pretty busy! This is why I'm giving you three different options, plus the reassurance that just pressing pause for 10 seconds throughout your day will make a difference too.

1. **I've only got 10 seconds: 1 x Calm Breath**
    10 seconds can make all the difference. Regular breaks of 10-second calm breathing may be all you can manage

as a new parent. This may be time for a deep, calm, conscious breath. Take one slow breath – stop, and be where you are in those 10 seconds. Hit the pause button. I suggest closing your eyes, but if you would rather keep them open, that's okay.

2. **I've got 1 minute: 10 x Calm Breaths**
   Stopping for regular breathing pauses, even for a just a minute, is shown to reduce anxiety and increase creative thinking. Even in the very early days of parenting, I used this all the time and I still do. When feeding, cooking or filling the car with fuel, waiting for the kettle to boil or rocking your baby, you can use a minute to take some calm breaths. As you get more used to doing the calm breaths, try saying in your mind: 'breathing in 3, 2, 1 … breathing out relax … relax … relax … ' At the end of each out-breath, pause, and allow yourself to notice what is in that moment.

3. **I've got 5 minutes: Listen to the Calm Breath track**
   If you do have longer, even if it's just 5 minutes, download and listen to the **Calm Breath** track so you can enjoy some 'me time'. You can do this before you go to sleep, when you are feeding, while your baby is contentedly playing or sleeping, when you are sitting at your desk, or even in the passenger seat of the car (with headphones on).

Daily self-care

Simple self-care can be a daily practice. Sometimes it may feel that baby is taking up all the space, and it can be hard to know how you can find the time for you. Taking moments to stop, slow down and do something for you will help to rest your mind, and make you feel nurtured and cared for. If you pay attention to your self-care, even if it's only for a minute here and there, cumulatively it will begin to make a real difference to how you feel. My clients say that they feel lighter, as if the sun is shining. You may not feel like this the very first time you try this exercise but give it time; it's a very subtle shift, but absolutely worth committing to.

EXERCISE 8: THE SELF-CARE RAINBOW

This self-care rainbow is designed for parents who are time poor. You choose 10 things to write on the rainbow that you love to do and make you feel great. It could be having a bath, getting your nails done, buying fresh strawberries, ringing a friend, crafting, having a glass of wine, going for a walk or even listening to your **Calm Breath**. It could take 10 seconds or 30 minutes; up to you! Colour in the rainbow, add glitter ... whatever makes it appealing to you! Nothing is too indulgent; this is an important part of your wellbeing and identity.

I stopped using the word 'indulging' and used the term 'embrace' instead. I'm not indulging in eating cake, having a long bath, walking by the river day after day on maternity leave, singing all day with my baby instead of doing housework; I am embracing being a mother and what I need to do.

Lola, mother to two children

Self-care rainbow

30 MINS

10 MINS

5 MINS

1 MIN

10 SECS

10 SECONDS

1 MINUTE

5 MINUTES

10 MINUTES

30 MINUTES

Summary

Acceptance, gratitude, affirmations, journaling, visualisation, goal setting, self-care and your **Calm Breath** are daily practices that you can integrate into your life. Any one of them is a chance to check in on yourself. If you just choose one for now, the **Calm Breath** can be used whenever you have a moment. I will remind you throughout the book to **PRESS PAUSE**, and take a **Calm Breath** or two.

You can join the Mindful Mamma Community online to get extra support and see how others have used and adapted these practices.

part two

Welcoming your Baby

3

Meeting your Baby

Suddenly you just know. It's time to start something new and trust the magic of beginnings.

Meister Eckhart

N o doubt you will be itching to tell family and friends, and
to take photos. But these first few moments and hours
after birth are so precious; they only happen once. **PRESS
PAUSE.** By noticing each detail of your baby, committing
the smell, the feel of their skin, the weight of them in your
arms for the first time, you open your heart up to imprinting
a memory, one that is deeper than a photograph will ever be.

When you meet your baby for the first time, you may feel
many things. The transition is almost impossible to describe,
as it's so different for everyone. No birth is the same, as no
woman's or parent's journey is the same. It is completely
normal at this stage to feel thrown into confusion. The physical and emotional changes are jostling for a place to be seen
and heard in a space that feels completely occupied with the
practicalities of caring for your baby.

That first explosion of love (or not)

Many women believe that the first moment you lay your eyes
on your baby you will feel this overwhelming feeling of love.

This may happen, or it may not. In either case, think of that love as an 'awakening'. It may develop over hours, days or weeks. This is true of every type of love. Sometimes love can be felt in small moments of intensity, like a candle flickering, coming and going until it stays on permanently. Even if you don't feel that love immediately, you would still protect that little person fiercely. That is a type of love too.

> The first time I saw my baby after a sudden and unexpected Caesarean birth, I felt nothing. I was shaking too much from the epidural to hold him, so my husband held him and I was simply glad he was okay. The following morning, I felt nothing much either but went through the motions. It was only the next day when I tucked him next to me in bed and his lovely little face gazed up at me that it hit me like a ton of bricks and I fell headlong in love with my tiny son and was totally smitten. If you don't get the 'golden hour' after birth, it doesn't mean that you won't bond. Sometimes it takes a little longer and that's okay.
>
> *Avril, mother to two children*

The minutes and hours after birth

We see some incredible images on social media of women after birth, powerful women who look as if they have taken on the world and won, women who are perfectly made up with lipstick and immaculate hair. Each image you see represents the story of the person who is behind that photo. A mother with her baby in theatre, or together in a birthing pool. They are not you, and you do not need to be any of those things. There are no expectations; you can choose to capture the moments after the birth in the way that is right for you. Or not at all. Remember that behind the photographs is the hustle and bustle of clearing up and tidying the room. Of practical things. You might want to have a shower and get dressed.

But first your baby. Before any of the photos, contacting your family and friends, take a moment to welcome your baby with all your heart and soul. **PRESS PAUSE.**

'I welcome you into the world with an open heart.'

Your baby may be in a normal state of adaptive stress after birth. Imagine emerging from your safe, quiet, warm abode into a world that is totally unfamiliar. Their body will surge with adrenaline; this helps mature their lungs, encouraging them to breathe. They have been in their own private swimming pool for nine months; their hair will be wet, and their body soft and slippery. There may be traces of blood on them and this is all normal. They may also be covered in creamy, white vernix, which can feel greasy. In fact, this is a great nutrient for your baby's skin.

Many midwives say after a short amount of time snuggling up, skin-to-skin, babies begin to soothe. Your voice, the touch of your skin, the smell of your milk, and the smell of amniotic fluid on their skin all help to calm your baby. This is the power of oxytocin, the hormone of labour and love. During the moments after birth a surge of oxytocin lights up the instinctive mothering part of your brain, preparing for the hours, days and weeks ahead. Oxytocin is amazing and is palpable in a room after a baby is born, affecting not just you but anyone else who is lucky enough to share in your experience. That's why it's called an 'oxytocin high'.

This first hour after the birth (sometimes called the 'golden hour') is an opportunity to just be with baby, as you are, with no expectation. Baby cannot see clearly yet, and hasn't seen you before, but they will be familiar with your sound and smell so let them rest in this familiarity.

> **Tip:** *Babies are soothed by music or audio tracks that you relaxed or listened to during pregnancy. The music becomes an association with their womb room. When baby is unsettled, you could try playing that music or tracks and see what happens.*

Your baby's new world

Sometimes we have to step inside someone else's shoes to know how their experience might be, and a hypnosis visualisation can help you to understand why these first moments are important for your baby. This visualisation will help you to connect with what your baby may experience, and help with your adjustment too.

Connect with your **Calm Breath** (see page 49) and imagine that you are resting with your eyes closed, somewhere warm and cosy. This might be in your home, snuggled up in your favourite blanket, or in your bed with the lights dim. You have some soft, soothing music on and your loved one is nearby. Imagine that suddenly your blanket is pulled off! It's cold, the lights are switched on, someone puts on some loud unfamiliar music, you call your loved one, but they are not there. You have no idea what is going on; it feels confusing and unsettling.

Now imagine if, when it was time to wake up, your loved one sat beside you and held you while your blanket was gently removed. The lights were not turned on immediately, but you were able to gently open your eyes in your own time. Your favourite music is playing softly in the background. The connection with your partner feels safe and soothing, and even though things are different, you have some moments to adjust.

Take a moment to say the following affirmation. You can say it as many times as you wish.

'I am glad you are here.'

EXERCISE 9: YOUR MAMMA AND BABY DEN

If the birth environment feels very busy and bright it can distract you in those early moments of saying hello to baby. This simple technique can help you to focus, wherever you are; it will help you to deepen your connection in the early moments. It can help you to focus on the details, committing them to memory and allowing those early connections to explode like fireworks in your and your baby's brains.

- You'll need a large lightweight shawl or blanket, but if you can't get one a sheet will do, or even a dressing gown. Improvise!
- Create a tent by draping it over you and your baby, and your partner too, if you like.
- Use your **Calm Breath** (see page 49). Breathing in, 3 … 2 … 1 … Breathing out, relax … relax … relax …
- Let go of any worries or busy thoughts, and just be where you are.

- Now really look at your baby. Notice their face, ears and eyes. See them deeply. With your finger, trace the shape of their face, ears and hands.
- Smell their head.
- Notice the weight of them in your arms.
- Stay in this moment for as long as you need.
- Whisper the following affirmation, if you like.

'As I breathe in I connect with you, as I breathe out I let go of everything else.'

> **Tip:** *You can use this technique long after the birth too, especially in any moment when you feel overwhelmed and want to focus on your baby without feeling watched or distracted.*

These moments, when your attention is deeply focused on baby, feel as if time slows down. In this space of 'slow awakening', reassurance can be found in the comfort of not needing to go anywhere or do anything. When you give birth, the changes in your brain and the fluctuation in your hormones accelerate. These powerful changes help you become responsive to your baby's cues; you'll instinctively learn when they need food, or changing, or just want a cuddle and to feel close to you. Finding ways to create a secure, safe space postnatally can help smooth this transition for your body and your mind.

Bringing calm into a busy birth

Whatever birth you have, you should have a chance for skin-to-skin contact to happen. As well as being soothing for your baby, it can be soothing for you too. It can act as a focus amidst disruption and whatever else is happening in the room. It will also release endorphins, your own natural painkillers.

Having had a baby prematurely I know how hard finding a moment for skin-to-skin can be sometimes, but as long as the people with you know that you would like this, they can help you to make this happen.

If you know you are having a Caesarean birth, you may be able to ask if the electrodes, which monitor your heart rate during the birth, can be placed on your shoulders and back. If not, don't worry, there will still be space for baby to rest on your chest.

Another lovely option is your partner holding baby; they could also sit next to you and you can hold your baby's hand and stroke their face. Even the touch of your baby's hand will make a difference, to you, and to your baby.

> **Tip:** *Be your baby's tailor-made incubator. Studies show that premature babies who were kept warm through continuous skin-to-skin contact enjoy long-term benefits to their health and wellbeing.*

My fourth baby, another Caesarean, but this time I planned it so I could have my baby girl skin-to-skin immediately. Holding her, smelling her, seeing her, feeling her was magical. I just couldn't stop staring at her. Her birth healed so much inside me, with the simple act of skin-to-skin.

Katie, mother to four children

Mindful presence not mobile absence

As your baby snuggles in your arms, you have the opportunity to imprint a memory, one that is deeper than a photograph will ever be. Take a photo by all means, but then put the phone away and sink into those moments, allow your baby and the moment to be as rich in detail as it can. This will be something to remember in the early weeks and right through parenthood.

Summary

Think 'slow awakening'. Keep the transition from womb to world, and from maiden to mother, as gentle as possible. Think about what you need to keep the room quiet, dark and uninterrupted after the birth. If you feel distracted, then use the baby den, your **Calm Breath** and your affirmation 'I am glad you are here' to welcome your baby with your whole heart. You can take all these techniques with you into the coming weeks and months, too.

4

The First Few Days

Life is a series of natural and spontaneous
changes. Don't resist them; that only creates
sorrow. Let reality be reality. Let things flow naturally forward in whatever way they like.

Lao Tzu

You may have given birth in hospital or at home. If you
had your baby in hospital you may be home for the
second or even first night. Sometimes it may be longer,
depending on the type of birth you had, and which hospital
you are in. If you are at home, your midwives will leave once
they see baby feeding, and you can snuggle up with your
new baby, partner and siblings, if you have other children.

Coming home from the hospital with our first son was a
moment when we realised that everything had changed; our
world had shifted. I remember standing in the sitting room
with our son, tiny in his snowsuit, strapped into his car seat.
My husband and I looked at each other and said in unison,
'What do we do now?' Somehow, we muddled through; we
got through that first day, then the second and the third. You
will too.

It can feel as if the practicalities of becoming a parent
mean there is no space left for anything else. If this is your
first baby, parenthood can be a sudden and steep learning
curve. Handling a newborn is an incredible experience;

their skin is unexpectedly soft, they seem so fragile and vulnerable, and it takes patience and presence to get to grips with feeling confident.

Tears will fall, however prepared you are.

> 'I am curious about the feelings that emerge in
> me, as I emerge into motherhood.'

Tears are a natural part of maternal adjustment and it happens to every woman. As your body and brain make the necessary changes to not being pregnant, there will be physical changes going on you are not even aware of consciously, and your body may do things that surprise you and which take your breath away. You may have thoughts that don't feel as if they belong to you, and the thoughts you do recognise may be amplified.

Leaning how to respond to those very early changes, moment by moment, can be something that you can learn to do before birth. It can be easy to feel overwhelmed when you have a new baby, but preparation can be key to recognising these early moments for what they are. Using the resources that you have within you, and between these pages, can help you to find the path forward that suits you best.

Your home is your nest

You can create a comfortable 'nest' wherever you choose; this could be your bed, your sofa, or somewhere else. It is somewhere that you can relax and let go. A nest is about protection, healing, and, in mammalian terms, safety and survival. This exercise will help you focus on where your nest should be, and what it needs.

EXERCISE 10: CREATING YOUR MAMMA NEST

Connect with your **Calm Breath**. Close your eyes and think about your home and the things that you are drawn to for comfort. There may be a specific blanket or pillow or a room that you love being in. If you are going to be spending the early weeks away from your home and somewhere else bring that into your mind. Ask yourself these questions and see what and who comes into your mind immediately. It has to be spontaneous and instinctive. You can write this in your journal as a reminder to yourself that you can always retreat to the comfort and safety of your nest.

- Where in my home do I feel most comfortable?
- Which things make me feel snug and comfortable?
- Who makes me feel comfortable?

The first nights at home

Those first nights after your baby has been born are not always easy. You may be very tired but not able to fall asleep. You may be in a baby bubble, just looking at this little person that you have waited months for, wanting reassurance that they are okay. It can feel familiar but unfamiliar at the same time. You may be in complete awe, and not be able to stop looking at them although your eyes just want to close – this is also an evolutionary response. Think about it; your instinct is primed to watch out for this vulnerable little human in the hours after birth.

'I will protect and care for you with gentle, loving kindness.'

Physically, your body is going through a lot, which can be difficult for sleep. You may be getting strong sensations in your
womb as it returns to its pre-pregnancy size. Your breasts will
be adapting to producing milk. If you have had a Caesarean birth
or any other type of intervention you may be on pain medication and have stitches. If you feel sore, slow down, and draw
your attention into your immediate awareness; we will do more
on this in Chapter 7, Healing and Renewal (see page 102).

*'I let go, slow down and accept
that my body needs time to adjust.'*

> **Tip:** *If you are having strong physical sensations
> use your* **Calm Breath** *to help relax. Breathe in 3 …
> 2 … 1 … breathe out relax … relax … relax … If you
> learned hypnobirthing techniques during pregnancy,
> do try these now as well.*

And your baby? The first night, baby may sleep; they may be
tired and still well-nourished from being fed by you through
your umbilical cord. After 24–48 hours, your baby may start
to notice hunger for the first time and that they aren't in their
womb room. They suddenly wake up.

Thinking about what it might be like to be your baby as
they make so many discoveries in such a short amount of
time can be a helpful way to adjust how you respond. It can
help to gently boost your compassion and patience in those
moments when you don't know what to do. Your baby
doesn't either! As the parent, at the very least *you* know

where you are, what sounds are around you, and what hunger is, so you are just who your baby needs to help them through this new stage in life.

EXERCISE 11: YOUR BABY'S WORLD

Close your eyes and imagine being your baby. Having never felt hungry before, you have these strange, uncomfortable sensations in your tummy. You might think: 'What is this unpleasant sensation?'

You suddenly discover you can make noise! 'What is that noise?'

And you cry without thinking about it:

'What is this sound I am making?'

'Where is that cosy, lovely warm womb, and heartbeat that made me feel soothed? And why can I stretch my arms out like this, there is so much space. It feels so different!'

Of course, baby doesn't think exactly this way yet; it's a purely primal response to get what they need to survive: food, warmth and safety. In this way nature is incredible. It may not seem so incredible at 3am, when you're a tired new mother and you don't know why your baby is crying or what to do about it. Instead, you may feel concerned that you aren't able to meet your baby's needs because you don't know how to. But you know what? You can do it, and you do know how. And if you don't right now, you are learning how. **PRESS PAUSE.**

From the very first day of parenthood, you are always learning, learning how to love and care for your baby. There will be practical challenges as well as emotional challenges. You will learn that it is normal for your baby to cry. It is normal for your baby not to sleep in the patterns that we have as adults. It is normal for your baby to want food when they feel hungry; if you are planning to breastfeed trust that your baby is going to be nourished in the first few days as your milk is coming in. The best thing that you can do is to accept that if a moment is tough it will pass, and it can help to connect with it deeply:

1. 'I accept the things I cannot change.'
2. 'Breathing in I let go, breathing out I soften.'
3. 'I know that I am doing all I can in this moment and that is enough.'
4. 'I give my mind and body permission to learn how to be a parent at a pace that is comfortable for me.'

The second night may be the steepest learning curve, and it can feel daunting. The reality is that every day you are learning more and more about how to parent your baby. Lean into it. If all you can do is wonder what to do, that's okay.

On day three, after my daughter was born, I remember telling my mum that I wanted someone to hit me over the head with a hammer – to knock me out just so that I could get some sleep. As soon as the words left my mouth, I felt so guilty about thinking such a thought, but I couldn't take it any longer. No-one had warned me about the heart palpitations I would get every time I closed my eyes; the moment I would drop off, my heart would jump as though I was being resuscitated and race like I'd never felt it do before. The night sweats left my skin feeling so soft but a softness I'd never felt before. I'd hear my little one crying, although she wasn't – I had this feeling that I couldn't sleep as no-one in the world would watch over her and keep her as safe as I could. This tiny little human being, that I'd created, that I'd longed for, was so precious and I had this overwhelming need to protect her.

By chance my husband had to work that evening so I packed my things and went to stay at my parents' house. My mum offered to come and stay at my house but even at the age of 28, there was something so comforting in going home, to the house where I grew up – I needed to be cared for and where better than the house I grew up in? While everything else felt so unfamiliar, my parents' house had that familiar smell and reassuring feeling of comfort that I needed. My mum offered to have my daughter's Moses basket in her room for the night; it wasn't easy but I felt as though I trusted my mum more than anyone else. She had 'been there' – she has raised me and my two siblings, she knew what she was doing. My mum brought my daughter to me each time she woke during the night for a feed but I did manage to sleep for a whole two hours straight; those two hours of solid sleep made the world of difference and I woke feeling refreshed, positive and much more like my normal self. I later learned that those feelings were very common and that the palpitations and night sweats were probably my body's way of releasing the adrenaline that had built up during my labour and stay in hospital.

Nichola, mother to two children

🎧 *You can start to listen to your **Confident Mamma** track in the days after baby is born. This will help you stay calm and reassured in those early days. This track may become very familiar to you, and you can continue to listen to it, and benefit from it, in the weeks and months to come.*

Summary

The first two days of parenthood are a rapid adjustment; moving from pregnant to not being pregnant is like a gear change. Take each moment as it comes. Keep the techniques as simple as you can: Create a nest, make yourself as comfortable as you can using the **Calm Breath**. Remember you are learning, your partner is learning, your baby is learning, any siblings are learning. Be kind and forgiving towards yourself.

5

The Fourth Trimester

No-one is ever quite ready; everyone is always
caught off guard. Parenthood chooses you.
And you open your eyes, look at what you've got,
say "Oh, my gosh," and recognise that of all the
balls there ever were, this is the one you should
not drop.

Marisa de los Santos

Once you have found your feet at home you are officially
in what is known as the fourth trimester. But what is
the fourth trimester and why does it matter?

It's the time after birth for healing, adaptation and transition. Traditions relating to it can be found all over the world. In some cultures, this time for bonding, recovery and connection is called 'lying in' or 'sitting the month'. It is called *La cuarentena* in Latin American Spanish, or *jaappa* in Hindi, and it can vary slightly in duration from around 22 days to 60 days.

One of the themes common to all traditions is warmth – a warm environment, warming food and warm, loving support. I have friends who have honoured their partner's culture by 'lying in' with the support of their mother-in-law. Although there were times when they were itching to get out and about, they say, in hindsight, how much they valued this time and how they recognised it as creating space for the mother in them to emerge. Mostly I hear from mothers who have done it with their second or third baby, having learned from the first time.

I used to call the fourth trimester my slow but fast stage. It felt so slow at times – when I was in it I couldn't see further than the end of that day. Despite that, the first 12 weeks flew by; I couldn't believe how fast things were moving on, and how much my baby was changing.

The fourth trimester can be seen as an extension of birth, a gentle emergence from the womb to the world for baby, and a time of adjustment to being not-pregnant again and becoming a mother for you. Your baby's birth was just the beginning.

Imagine the transition from pregnancy to motherhood as a wobbly bridge. You have to hold on, with one hand, because you have a baby in the other, watching each and every step carefully with intense focus. It can feel like you are holding your breath, you may feel as if you are completely winging it, and sometimes the slats on the bridge don't feel very stable at all. But you *will* get to the other side. You will never move backwards – some days all you can do is hang on, regain your balance, and breathe. Other days you will be able to move forward enjoying the view. Whatever kind of day it is, keep moving forwards with an open heart and trust that your parenting will become as natural as putting one foot in front of the other. **PRESS PAUSE.**

It's all I have to bring today—
This, and my heart beside—
This, and my heart, and all the fields—
And all the meadows wide—

Emily Dickinson

There are so many experiences, emotions and feelings that happen in these early months and it can be intense. It's definitely not a linear experience; every aspect of the fourth trimester – your baby, thoughts, feelings, body, relationships, exhaustion, feeding, identity – seem to be present in each moment, interconnected as a whole. Learning how to respond to these new experiences and feelings now will put you in great stead not just for the first year, but beyond that.

There is so much to learn emotionally and physically. Not all the changes you experience are visible; your brain is busy going through a physical upgrade, reorganising and prioritising aspects of itself that will help you raise your child. This is about species survival. It's your biology.

Media portrayals of perfectly put-together new mothers create cultural expectations of how you should look or act in the first few weeks after birth, for example, 'getting up and about as soon as possible' or 'getting your body back'. These kinds of expectations can try to bulldoze biology, but biology needs to be heard and respected, especially in the early stages of motherhood.

Perhaps think about this fourth trimester as a large room full of new paperwork and instruction manuals that have just been delivered, piles of paper everywhere. You have to understand it first to organise it, know where to file it so you can retrieve it easily, then finally you can start using the information efficiently. Give yourself time and space to do this by slowing down when you can, and prioritising the basic needs of you and your baby. This will give your brain energy to make sure everything is in place before it starts firing on all cylinders again.

To sort this you need
Time and space

'I am/we are creating a strong foundation for the years ahead.'

Second time round, I was prepared. I knew how hard the fourth trimester could be and that I needed to accept it, ride with it, accept my feelings and not try to fight them or hide them. Not put on a front or 'bounce back' as I thought I had been expected to do the first time around. I knew it was important to take things slowly this time round, for the sake of my daughter, who needed to adjust to life as a big sister, too. The first week home, we didn't have any visitors and I lived in my pyjamas. I had thought about doing this the first time around but think we were so excited and proud to show our first born off that we had visitors from the moment we arrived home and, in my opinion, it definitely hindered my recovery.

This time, I focused on resting and knew that we could still enjoy showing our little one off to friends and family, but just a few days later. Staying in pyjamas and cancelling all plans for the week meant there was no pressure. I slowed my pace of life right down, I didn't even leave the house for four days straight. This would normally drive me crazy but I loved every moment: trying to live in the moment, soaking up all those newborn cuddles, listening to my body, sleeping when I felt the need to sleep, crying when I felt the need to cry. I'd batch-cooked my favourite comfort meals before baby arrived so didn't have to worry about cooking. My mum and sister called each day to ask if we needed anything from the shops, so we didn't even need to leave the house for supplies. We tried to keep some normality for my daughter, so my husband took her to her pre-school sessions and toddler classes as normal. This gave me extra time to rest, sleeping when baby slept (something I learned is possible and so valuable). I had given myself permission before baby arrived that for one week I wouldn't worry about cleaning the house; I usually followed The Organised Mum Method cleaning schedule but knew this was unrealistic with a newborn so made it explicit to myself and my husband that I would take at least one whole week off. I gradually re-introduced my level 1 jobs over the next few weeks and the other levels would come back in when I felt ready, much later in my fourth trimester.

Nicola, mother to two children

Parenthood is open 24/7

You'll learn very quickly that parenthood is open 24 hours a day, 7 days a week for all baby essentials: milk, nappy changing, reassurance, warmth and comfort. You can't put a closed sign on the door to parenting.

In those moments when you want to put a closed sign up, you can make a choice to accept the experience, and surrender to it. Using the term 'surrender' may make it seem as if you are coming through a battle, and some days it can feel like an internal conflict between what you want to do for yourself and what you get to do with your baby. However, they are not moments to battle or defeat but to acquiesce to. Surrendering to the need to stay in bed all day with your baby if you are too tired to do anything else is a powerful choice that you can make for your wellbeing.

Pause for a moment, and connect with your **Calm Breath** where you are. Now think about how there are some things you can change and some you can't. Give yourself permission to let go of the things you can't change. You can use this affirmation as a reminder to yourself throughout the first year, as you face new challenges.

'I accept and let go of the things I cannot change.'

When they can't change things, I've heard mothers describe a feeling of hopelessness. Hopelessness can seem such a negative word, when in fact it can be transformational. This can mean that even though your soul is willing, what you are expected to do may seem impossible.

A feeling of hopelessness can be a space of intense personal development and connection, with yourself, your partner and your baby. When you look back at how capably you were able to make the good and strong choices when you felt hopeless, you'll learn how something powerful can arise from within that space. My son had chronic reflux, right up until he was one. I felt a sense of hopelessness feeding him, as it would come straight up as projectile vomit, but I carried on feeding and cleaning. At times I wondered why I did, but something in me wouldn't give up. My instinct to continue was right; one day in that space I realised the moments while I was feeding him were priceless and far outweighed the stress of cleaning it all up. It also brought my husband and me closer as we faced the challenge together.

'I am growing into hopefulness each and
every day.'

The rhythm of the night

> **Tip:** *Use your* **Calm Breath** *to stay afloat, and to find mini-pauses throughout the night and day. Connecting with your breath can be a reminder to surrender to the moment you are in.*

It may feel sometimes as if the days are merging into the nights and that the comfortable rhythm of your daily cycle has been turned on its head. Some mothers describe the nights as hard and tiring, and others, especially second-time mothers, quickly learn to recognise that this is part of caring for a newborn. You can decide how to make this stage the best you can. One way to think about it, if you have other children, is that this may be one of the few times you get to spend with your new baby without interruption. It's exhausting and hard work, but you can do it. Take it feed by feed, and night by night.

Accept that your wellbeing isn't based on the circadian rhythm you are used to; instead, accept that you are on baby rhythm for a while. Rather than night sleep, you will adapt to pockets of sleep and rest. We will explore how to manage this more in Chapter 12, Rest and Sleep, on page 170.

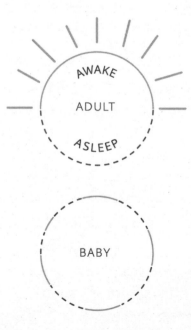

If you need to be awake during the night, find or create a comfy space to be. This could be your bed, or elsewhere somewhere else that you can comfortably recline. Rest with your baby somewhere safe and doze, allowing your mind rest in those half-waking moments of the night. You may be interested in exploring the benefits of and research on co-sleeping at this point.

You can stick up a note near your comfy space to act as a reminder to switch off and accept that in those early hours you are soothing baby and giving them everything they need.

'Let us wrap the night around us and rest in love and tranquillity.'

🎧 Listen to the **Dynamic Sleep** track as baby is feeding to boost the rest you are getting.

The fourth trimester isn't something I really knew about when I initially became a mum. I entered pregnancy and motherhood with an 'ignorance is bliss' attitude towards everything from birth to baby. Looking back, I wish I'd read and researched more, so I could have really appreciated the first 12 weeks of my eldest daughter's life – and given myself more of a break! Instead I felt constantly overwhelmed and put so much pressure on myself to get back to normal, not really understanding how much my 'normal' had changed.

However, I'm now three children in, and I now know that, although tough and thoroughly exhausting, this period of time is wonderful and sacred; they're only a newborn for such a small amount of time. It's a cliché for a reason – they do grow up so fast.

That doesn't stop it being overwhelming of course; there have been numerous times over the past 12 weeks when I've been so utterly exhausted that I've sobbed into my lukewarm coffee, not knowing how I was going to get through the rest of the day. But when you also have a six-year-old and a three-year-old running around, it gives you a real sense of perspective, and reassurance that you *will* sleep again, because it won't be like this forever (I remember the first time round; it truly felt never-ending!)

The fourth trimester is full of magical moments and milestones. There are the first cuddles, the first smiles, sometimes the first giggles, and the first poonami (okay, maybe that's not a brilliant milestone, but once you've tackled a nappy explosion that also covers the car seat as well as your baby, you can deal with pretty much anything!). You learn how skilled you are at doing things one-handed. How powerful oxytocin, adrenaline and love can be to keep you going. How strong you really are as a person, but also how vulnerable motherhood can leave you.

Every experience, every feeling, every emotion is valid. Having a baby is a huge, relentless, daunting upheaval. Everything has changed. You have brought a life into the world. Your body is covered in marks that weren't there before: both visible and not.

One of my favourite things about the fourth trimester? This time round I've strung fairy lights up around our bed to help me see during night feeds. Making eye contact in the early hours of the morning under the glow of the fairy lights, when the rest of the house is fast asleep and silent, is magical. It's an excellent example of how motherhood is a bombardment of contrasting feelings: those 3am night feeds are relentless and exhausting, but they're also fleeting and wondrous. Oh, the power of love, hormones and coffee.

Hannah Harding, mother to three children

Tip: *Avoid the perils of 3am shopping roulette and a stream of packages you can't remember buying. Instead, switch your phone off and take that time to just sit in stillness and rest your mind. You can use the sensory spotlight on page 123 to help with this.*

A stream of visitors

Support is really important for new parents, but it's also careful to not feel overwhelmed in the first weeks, and have space to find your feet.

Everybody will want to see and hold your baby. Many of your family and friends will have shared your journey with you and can't wait to meet baby. It's fine for you to ask them to put the brakes on, choosing who you invite into your home and when. You and your baby are not a human zoo; you don't have to be open for visitors all the time.

You may be very willing and ready to show your baby off, or you may want to create a pocket of time to bond together with your partner and baby. Views are mixed on this, but the intensity of experience can mean that there are lots of unexpected feelings in these early days such as fragility and vulnerability. You may feel quite fiercely protective of your baby, uncomfortable passing them around, or you may feel very comfortable with this. It is so individual. Really listen to what your body and your heart is telling you.

> I didn't mind other people holding our new baby at visits. It was the immediate time after birth I struggled with. I wanted privacy to meet our son. We had a hospital birth with an early discharge so we could get comfortable at home. I found that family was confused by the concept of early discharge from hospital, so we were followed into our driveway by eight family members eager to meet baby. I hadn't slept yet and this made the first couple of nights at home a really tough adjustment. I will vocalise my wishes more if we have another child. Sleep is precious, as was the bond forming between mamma, baby and dad in the fourth trimester.
>
> *Danielle, mother to one child*

Saying no to visitors may be hard for you, but always put your and baby's needs at the centre. It can be easy to say no to some people, but how can you say no to people who you know want to be supportive and kind, who you love and care about? Here's how:

EXERCISE 12: CREATING A SAFE SPACE

This hypnosis visualisation will help you to connect with the part of you that is ready, or not ready, for visitors. It can help you to connect with your intuition and vulnerability in a positive and powerful way, and to sharpen your intuition listening skills! Be aware that sometimes your intuition can be felt as a subtle physical tightening in the solar plexus (the area just above your belly button). Tune into your intuition and notice how the feeling or energy changes in that area.

1. Close your eyes. Take a deep breath in and connect with what you are feeling now. Your baby, your body, the space you are in, and your level of comfort.
2. Now imagine visitors coming into your space.
3. If it's a particular person, imagine them.
4. How do you feel? Do you feel comfortable with them being there? Is it tiring, are they helpful, do they impose, or are they respectful? How does it feel with them holding the baby?
5. Open your eyes. If you are happy with what you felt, let them in for real, but be aware of what your boundaries are. You may enjoy having them there, but not be ready for them to hold baby yet. It's all up to you. Let your intuition guide you.

MASTERING THE ART OF SAYING NO

If you are not ready to invite people into your home, you can say 'no' in lots of different ways. Research shows that if you use the word 'because', people are more likely to agree and accept your reasoning.

Try these phrases if your head is foggy and you are worried about upsetting someone:

- Thank you for being there for me. I'm really looking forward to seeing you in a few days/next week because you are going to love [insert baby's name].
- Thanks for your kindness, it means a lot because we are really enjoying spending some time getting to know our baby. Let's get a date in for when things are more settled because I'd love to spend some proper time with you.
- I'm so tired today because we're getting to grips with [feeding/had a tough night/spending some quiet time], so let's rearrange.

On the flipside, visitors can be very helpful, by bringing shopping, helping out with meals and housework. Don't forget to have fun! Think of your friends; it can be lovely having them pop by – love and laughter can be a welcome guest. Knowing who are the right people to have in your space can help; you can do this by asking yourself these questions. If you don't feel comfortable enough asking them to do these things, then perhaps they aren't the person to have in your space right now:

- Can I ask them to bring some shopping round?
- Do I feel comfortable asking them to make their own tea?
- Can I ask them to hang the washing out?
- Can I ask them to cook me a meal?
- How are they helping me?

One of the kindest things was by a former neighbour of mine, Jeanie, who had produced a gorgeous CD of tracks for me to listen to. She popped round to see how I was doing when my husband went back to work and stayed for a short amount of time. She herself was on maternity leave, about to have her baby, and it was such a thoughtful thing to do – I've always remembered this simple gesture. The perfect guest!

Alice, mother to two children

Postnatal doula

You may want to consider a postnatal doula. Usually a mother herself, this is someone who is trained to support you emotionally and practically during the fourth trimester. They have trained in breastfeeding support too, and can help with nights. Many friends of mine have asked for a post-natal doula instead of gifts for baby. Some postnatal doulas are termed 'mentored', which means that they have trained but need more experience to qualify. This can be more affordable as they may only charge expenses; what a great exchange! You can find out more at www.doula.org.uk.

EXERCISE 13: BRING IT BACK TO BASICS

You don't have to do everything at once. It may be hard to sit there and watch the pile of ironing grow, or the plates stack up in the sink, but at times you need to preserve your energy. On a high-energy day, you can download this as a worksheet and have a copy on the wall at home. On days you have no spare energy, stick to items in list 1. Think of it as a forgiving 'to do' list!

Lower-energy days

Eg. Stay in bed, walk to the bathroom and back

....

....

....

....

Mid-energy days

Eg. Get up, get dressed, walk around the block

....

....

....

....

High-energy days

Eg. Get up, get dressed, walk around the block
and tackle some washing

....

....

....

....

1. If you are exhausted and don't feel like doing anything, think about the absolute basics that you need to do to care for yourself, baby and any other children. It may be having a shower, eating, drinking, and having a cuddle with your other children in front of a film.
2. What would you prioritise if you had a little more energy and could do something more than the basics? Maybe some washing, or a bit of cleaning, or do an online shop?
3. On days when you are feeling more energetic think about what you can do with the energy: Go to the shops, take your baby and other children to the park. Or perhaps prepare a batch of food ready for days when you feel exhausted.

> **Tip:** *People love lists, so be practical and specific about what you want help with and write it down. If people ask if they can help, get them to choose something from the list!*

When Sylvia was born (given that I often feel over-whelmed by things) we kept the amount of physical stuff in the house to the absolute minimum we could manage. Changing tables, monitors, digital play mats, bouncers, baby swings, all the tech we are scared into buying. Both the financial pressure and the space they take up are fundamentally stressful and I found it really important that our space still felt ours. I wanted it defined by us as people, rather than the whole house being taken over by this new being. When it came to it she was just as happy lying in a washing basket with a folded blanket. I think sometimes we can believe that all the stuff you can buy will be armour through these scary times but it can actually end up being an expensive shackle and make you feel a stranger in your own home.

Holly, mother to one child

Managing a time of extremes

One minute you may feel fine, and completely on top of everything, the next you may feel as if you aren't doing enough at all. Being a parent in those early days can be a mixed bag. As well as love, joy and contentment, you may also experience feelings of ambivalence, frustration and resentment. All of these feelings are valid and can be completely normal in the weeks after birth. Consider times in your life when you have made other major transitions and changes; how have you felt about those?

'The more I accept this period of change, the easier it is for me to create balance.'

Using existing coping mechanisms is something that can really benefit you. Not only do they feel familiar, but you are already conditioned to using them. In the thick of the fourth trimester, it can be easy to forget what they are, or to call them into your mind. Having them written down means that you can reference them quickly and easily. Take a moment now, use your **Calm Breath** and connect with that space within you. Allow memories to come up with ways that you have navigated tough feelings and emotions in the past. It may have been quiet space, chatting to a friend, fresh air … Think of things that you can do with a baby, or think creatively about how you can adapt them. Write them here:

1.

2.

3.

DOES SOCIAL MEDIA HELP OR HINDER YOU?

Social media can both help you and challenge you in the fourth trimester. An explosion in social media means that images of birth and postnatal experiences are at your fingertips 24 hours a day. It can be hugely reassuring to find other women experiencing the same things as you, and it can help you build an online community of support. The flipside is the prevalence of a culture that holds up unrealistic expectations of what is achievable in those early days.

Write down three reasons why social media helps you:

Write down three reasons why it doesn't help you:

With these thoughts in mind, think about adjusting how you use social media. You might decide to have days when you set yourself the challenge of switching off completely.

Summary

The fourth trimester is a time of very early adjustment. Create your nest and spend plenty of time where you feel supported and comfortable. It's okay for your PJs to be your best friend! Accept that life is different, and get to know it in a different way. Relax into slow parenting, familiarising yourself with your baby's cues. Give your mind and body time to adjust and rebalance itself; remember, it's just 12 weeks of a whole lifetime. Give yourself permission to accept the challenges, enjoy the magic of your baby awakening to themselves, and lean into the intensity of the experience.

6

Getting to Know your Baby

Let tenderness pour from your eyes, the way sun
gazes warmly on the earth.

Hafiz

During the first few days of your baby arriving, allow your baby's details to sink in. Look at their face, hair, limbs and eyes; you will be building a connection in your mind with your baby, and your ancestors. Who do they look like? The people who they come from will shape how they *look*, but you, your partner and the people around you will help shape how they *are*.

This tiny human will grow and change so quickly. It may not seem it at first, as things seem to go so slowly sometimes, but this time will pass by quickly. One day you'll look back and be astonished at how quickly your baby has adapted and grown into the world around them. Not just in how they communicate, but also in how they look. **PRESS PAUSE.**

'I am taking time to sit and notice the changes in you each and every day.'

You already know so much about your baby by the time they are born; you have formed a connection while still in your womb. You may have sung to your baby, spoken to them, had conversations with them. You have felt or seen them kick, you may have heard them speak to you unconsciously, perhaps when you had a conversation with them you automatically filled in their answers. But before they were born, you had never heard your baby's voice or smelt or felt their skin; you have only seen the outline of their body as they moved in your belly, or the blurry outline of them on a scan. So now is the time to get to know your baby better.

Looking at Maggie for the first time I felt I was transported into another world, a little like labour, yet deeper. I felt I understood 'mystery' and yet understood nothing at the same time. I just felt all this LOVE like no other. The first time I saw Tove I was more alert. I was still laughing (a technique used for labour). I, again, instantly loved her and felt a huge relief with this as I couldn't imagine loving another as much as I did Maggie. I felt my heart grow in a flash. When I looked at Tove I felt wisdom and earthy, very grounded. And now at the age of four and a half, nobody makes me laugh more.

Lola, mother to two children

In those early weeks you can lay the foundations of connection and communication between you and baby. This is one of the most important things early on – getting to know your baby, and letting them get to know you, before introducing them to others. This could be the most important meeting of your life, so shut the world out, tuck yourselves up, and learn to know deeply this gorgeous human being who you are going to share the rest of your life with.

EXERCISE 14: BREATHE-BABY-CONNECT

This is a colour visualisation that will help you to use your breath to connect with your baby. Colours are used a lot in hypnosis as they carry the resonance of feelings. Everyone has the capacity to relate colour to feeling. If I were to ask you to think of a colour that makes you feel calm, what would it be? This is very simple and can be used anywhere, at any time, even if you are not with your baby at that time, and want to reconnect. It is also useful if you are ever in a situation where you need to stay calm with baby.

Close your eyes and use the **Calm Breath** (see page 49), use breathing in, 3 ... 2 ... 1 ..., breathing out, relax ... relax ... relax ... to fall into your comfortable rhythm.

- Now imagine that as you are breathing in, you breathe in a colour that is calming to you.
- As you breathe out, imagine breathing out that calming colour.
- Then imagine your baby breathing it in.
- As your baby breathes out, you breathe in.
- Imagine that calming colour as a thread becoming a circular breath between you and your baby.

Tip: *If you really get on with this breathing exercise, you might like to wear a bracelet or a wrist band in the colour you have chosen. If you feel anxious or disconnected it can be a gentle reminder to connect to your breath and your baby.*

Tune into your baby

By really looking at your baby with focused attention, you will be able to tune into your baby's frequency, noticing the way that they respond to you and their environment. Even though your baby can't speak yet, they are developing new ways of responding to their environment each and every day. When you take the time to sit or lie down with them, and really notice them, you will begin to see patterns emerging in how they communicate. Just watching your baby and being with them is enough right now.

You may wonder, what will your baby be like when they're older? What will their hobbies will be? Will they be a reader, a traveller, an entertainer, love sports or science, or all or none of those things? Instead of thinking about who they might be, I encourage you to focus on who they are right now. I often found myself absently wondering who my children would turn out to be, when who they are is right in front of me every moment of every day. Inevitably, neither of them was interested in what I expected them to be interested in, and they surprise me every day, because they are completely unique individuals. If you find yourself wondering the same thing, say this:

'I am glad that you are you.'

Who they are now is not who they will be tomorrow, or the day after that. Your baby will always be changing. Connect with and love who they are right now. See them and celebrate every part of them. Being accepted and seen for who they are is something your baby will benefit from even in these early weeks but even more so as they grow and become more independent.

EXERCISE 15: A WINDOW TO YOUR BABY'S SOUL

This mindfulness exercise helps you to set time aside just to do nothing else but connect and notice your baby. This is focused attention. When you do this you are doing so much. You are allowing yourself to be present without distraction, and your baby is getting the benefit of wholehearted connection. When you see your baby deeply, you are being attentive, you are building pathways of communication, affection and empathy that are the foundation for the future. It is helpful to try this when neither of you is distracted and when you and baby are awake and settled, so your baby can be present with this connection too. Mornings are usually the best time.

Start with just one minute, but you may want to do it for longer as you get used to it. Perhaps set time aside for it at a certain time every day; if it becomes a habit, it becomes a practice that is easier to keep up.

> 'Breathing in I am with you, breathing out I let
> go of everything else.'

- Smile at your baby.
- Say: 'In this moment, I let go and connect with you deeply.' You can say this silently, or softly out loud.
- Look into and notice your baby's eyes. Look deeply into their eyes. If your baby looks away, notice where their gaze goes.
- Notice and explore the depth of colours in their eyes. Name the different colours in their eyes.
- Notice their eyelashes.
- Trace your thumbs over their eyebrows, noticing how they feel and how your baby responds to that touch.

- Notice how you are responding to this. Observe that feeling, let it go and return your attention to your baby. If you feel impatient or your thoughts start wandering, just come back to your breath.

> **Tip:** *You might like to try this with any older children you have. Why not suggest if they can see how many colours they can count in your eyes?*

Being aware of your baby's space

You will be aware of your baby's physical presence at a conscious level. You can look at your baby right now and say, 'I see you, I know you are there.' You can also become aware of your baby in your space energetically – this is more of an unconscious sense of your baby being in the space around you.

Close your eyes, **PRESS PAUSE**, connect with your **Calm Breath** and just be aware of your baby right now and where they are now, noticing the space between you and where they are, and the space between you and where they are not.

EXERCISE 16: THE SPACE YOU SHARE

Taking some time to really focus on your baby's presence can help you to become more aware of the space that baby occupies, and to know that you are always connected somehow. It becomes a sixth sense, knowing where your baby is! You can try this exercise at different times over the coming days and months; notice if your response to it changes and how.

- Lie down on the floor with your baby placed safely about an arm's length on your right side.
- Close your eyes, and take a deep breath, connecting with your breathing.
- Notice where your baby is lying, and notice how the space is between you and your baby.

Now shift your attention to the space above you, noticing how that is. Now shift your attention to your left, noticing how that is. And below. Now back to your baby on your right, noticing how that is again. How is that space? Is it different for you?

Tip: *You can try this when your baby is with your partner, a relative or childminder. Explore the space around you when your baby is not in your home with you and notice how it changes.*

Summary

Take time to get to know your baby. Nurture that connection by focusing on their appearance and their mannerisms. Really *see* them, noticing the details. Familiarise yourself with the space that you and baby occupy together. Learn to feel the connection you have wherever you and your baby are.

7

Healing and Renewal

Be still and heal.

Thich Nhat Hanh

In the past year you have gone from being not pregnant, to being pregnant, giving birth and having a baby. Wow!

Your body has done something magnificent. Whichever way you birthed your baby, you created this little person. Give yourself a high five! To do this, your body had to make many significant physical changes, and in the first 12 weeks after birth will be shifting back to where it was. You will need some time to heal and adapt; your body may be sore, and may ache. Your brain is also adapting and changing, something that we don't really think about, but is felt intensely through the ups and downs of feelings and emotions.

Your experience is unique to you; you may need to heal more or less than other women. Your womb has had the mother of all workouts; it's a muscle that has been working hard and you wouldn't expect to wake up the next day after a hard workout at the gym without any aches, would you? Your breasts may be tender and sore, you may be getting used to breastfeeding, and even if you have chosen not to, your breasts will still be leaking at moments that you least expect them to in those early weeks.

'I slow down, and allow myself to recover in heart, body and mind.'

You may have stitches that feel uncomfortable and sore. Having the first poo after birth can create some apprehension, which may create tension. In this case, use your **Calm Breath** (see page 49). Relax your shoulders, relax your hands. Release as much tension in your body as you can.

> **Tip:** *You can use a hypnosis visualisation to help with discomfort and pain. Imagine a dial in your head that turns down pain in your body. Notice where it is set, then as you breathe, imagine turning it down. It may turn down slowly or quickly. Keep doing it until you notice a difference.*

Gratitude for your amazing body

As well as physical healing, you are also getting to know this little person, adjusting to motherhood, and finding your feet in a changed world. If there was ever a time to be kind to your body, this is the time. Your body is amazing and learning to love it for what it has done can be transformative. Say to your body:

'Thank you for growing my baby and doing everything you did to bring baby into the world.'

Healing from the inside out

Healing is often associated with being ill, and not with pregnancy, because pregnancy isn't an illness. Our culture needs to shift its thinking on postnatal care. If you have had assistance with your baby's birth, whether forceps, ventouse or a Caesarean birth, you have had a medical intervention. For any other medical intervention like this you would rest and recover, wouldn't you? Why not for birth? Allow your body the space and time it needs to rebalance and repair itself, and for you to be as comfortable as you can. When you are physically comfortable, somehow you have more capacity for the other challenges that will arise in the coming months. If you have had intervention, learn about the practical things you can do help you to recover. There are some resources that I've signposted you to in the back of the book (see page 267).

> Frozen pads are a lifesaver! Douse night-time sanitary towels in aloe vera, arnica and tea tree oil and then freeze ready for when you return home from the hospital post-birth.
>
> *Kym, mother to one child*

EXERCISE 17: SOOTHING VISUALISATION

Coolness can be numbing and soothing, and hypnosis visualisations using cool imagery can be helpful if you have any physical discomfort in your body. The more you practise this, the more effective it gets. You'll find you start to do it automatically as well.

- Imagine that it's a very cold winter's day. There is deep snow around you.
- Close your eyes and imagine standing outside in the freezing cold with bare feet. It's so cold you can see your breath, and you may also be shivering. Imagine

your feet becoming numb, and that cold numbness moving up through your legs and into your belly.
- Imagine guiding that numbing coolness into whichever part of your body you choose as you breathe in. Draw up that cool feeling into your body and move it into any part of your body that needs it.

Research shows that you can influence your experience of pain through your thoughts and can even direct pain relief to different parts of your body. Hypnosis visualisations can harness this power and are a great tool in helping you manage discomfort and pain – allowing you to be comfortable with discomfort. They are really powerful, and I use them even when I have minor surgery. Many women I work with use visualisation successfully. One woman imagined 'knitting nannies' knitting her womb and muscles back together!

To the bemusement of the midwives I used all my hypnosis techniques after the birth for when I had stitches. I declined the local anaesthetic and used my visualisations and breathing. I breathed in the oxytocin while cuddling my baby ... everything I needed was in my mind. I felt amazing in those moments, and it showed me how powerful the tools I had learned are.

Anna, mother to two children

Visualisation works along similar lines to the placebo effect. We know from research that if you are told you are going to receive medication to help with discomfort or pain, it can actually bring down the pain levels in your body. This is true even if you *know* that the 'medication' you are receiving is a placebo. I've always seen hypnosis as a form of 'ethical placebo' – people come to see me and want to use hypnosis because they know, and believe, that the power of their mind can change their experience, both physically and emotionally.

> 'I trust that my thoughts are powerful and can create changes in how I feel and heal.'

Even more interesting is that studies are now beginning to explore how hypnosis and meditation can accelerate healing. Mostly studies have been focused on areas such as post-operative wound-healing. One, remarkably, showed how using hypnosis improved vasodilation in burns recovery – this means that blood pressure was reduced, and blood and oxygen flow to the wound site increased, helping it to heal faster. **PRESS PAUSE.**

By reducing stress and increasing opportunities to relax, as well as actively using hypnosis visualisation techniques, you are doing everything you can to support your body to heal in the shortest time it is able.

EXERCISE 18: THE LANGUAGE OF HEALING

This exercise can be used to tap into the power of your imagination and your mind. You're going to unlock the powerful language of the unconscious: its colours, shapes and images. You don't have to tell anyone what comes up for you in your mind, just go with it. It's very simple and, I always find, fun to do.

You can use this every day, or when you have a moment. You can do it lying in the bath, on the sofa, in bed before you sleep or when you are holding your baby.

- Take a deep breath. Allow your shoulders to soften and your breath to settle into a comfortable rhythm.
- Close your eyes and focus on the sensation or discomfort in your body that you want to ease.
- Now give that sensation a colour, shape or symbol. Allow what comes into your mind. Remember that your imagination is magical and limitless.
- If you were to change that colour, shape or symbol so it disappears completely and for good, what would you have to do to it?
- Use whatever comes into your mind that helps change that feeling. When it begins to change, keep going.
- Keep going until that feeling is gone or significantly softened.

An alternative here is to use a healing colour:

- If there were a colour that could heal what would it be?
- As you breathe in, breathe that colour down into the area that needs healing.
- Imagine it repairing, healing.

Personally, I used visualisation when I broke my elbow. I fell over holding one of the boys, unglamorously on the pavement outside my mother-in-law's house. I imagined that I had Snow White and the Seven Dwarfs in my elbow every day, smoothing edges away and polishing the bone. I imagined my elbow at full extension, and I visualised a golden, healing light, filling the bone crack, like *Kintsugi*. My consultant congratulated me on resting it (the boys were six months old and two years old at the time!) and said he'd rarely seen an elbow bone heal so fast or with full extension.

It's an anecdotal story, but I use this technique all the time, and with other people, with great success. It may be a powerful placebo, but it's great fun, it's free and it can be used anywhere at any time.

Healing your mind

The mind and body are intrinsically connected. Birth can be experienced differently by many people; what may seem like a straightforward birth may be experienced traumatically for one woman, while another woman could have a birth full of intervention and not be traumatised by it. Whatever experience you have had is valid, however your baby's birth unfolded. Coming to terms with disappointment around your baby's birth, or any associated trauma, may take time and will need the right support.

While the techniques explained earlier are perfect for allowing you to take an active part in your physical healing process, when it comes to your thoughts and feelings, you may need to take a slightly different approach.

'I know that I made the best decisions I could with the information and knowledge I had.'

If you are feeling traumatised, upset, or feeling your body has failed you, I'm sorry that this is the experience you have had, and are having. Talking therapies are often a restorative way to explore your thoughts and feelings and there are several different ways to do this. In some units a 'birth reflection' service is offered, and you might want to try this. Some research suggests that this does not always make a difference; this may be because it doesn't feel safe or comfortable to go back to a unit, or to a team, connected with the trauma.

Many of the health professionals I speak to agree that for the reflection to be of value you have to do it where you feel safe and heard. Importantly, you have to have a good rapport and feel comfortable and safe with the person you are speaking to. Alternatives to birth reflections can be through your GP, or via self-referral to a psychology service. Self-referral is only offered in some places so you will need to ask your GP surgery if it's an option in your area. You can also choose to see a doctor, therapist or a psychologist privately. There are also charities that you can speak to (see page 267).

Rewind Technique can be a very quick and effective way of processing trauma. It's a psychological tool that uses hypnosis; it can help you to process trauma with a reduced risk of re-traumatisation. There are psychologists and therapists offering this service both in the NHS and privately. See if someone with this specific training is practising near you and if this is something that you may be interested in.

'I trust that my body did the best that it could do.'

I have spoken to many women who tell me they feel that their body failed them in some way. If this resonates with you, know that your body *didn't* fail you; your body, and you, did the best you could. All the women I see give everything they have to birth their baby; this is primal intention. Yes, we learn that birth is natural, but sometimes nature needs help. I want you to pause for a moment and shift your lens. Shift it to what your body *did* do. I want you to think about conception, pregnancy, how your body grew your baby, as well as the birth. Now write down three amazing things your body did to bring your baby to you:

1.

2.

3.

The first time I saw my baby I felt euphoric and exhausted! I had just given birth after four hours in a pool. I had a retained placenta and shortly after my calm birth I was taken to theatre to have a manual removal. I went through the decision process thoughtfully. I also used 3...2...1...relax when having my epidural. In the days and weeks following my birth I had a lot of guilt around the hour or so that I was separated from my baby. My hubby and sister said she did nothing but cry! I felt for a long time that my sister could settle my baby better and used to think that she preferred her to me as she'd spent those first few hours earth-side with her. I used to think that my baby thought my sister was her mummy. I had to talk to my sister and husband about this a lot, to process my feelings of guilt, and also be kind to myself. I used mindfulness breathing when feeling overwhelmed with guilt. I also practised gratitude that I had my calm birth, and I never let the retained placenta be the focus of my birth – my birth was serene and magical and the afterbirth was a small part that didn't go to plan, but it didn't define my birth.

Hannah, mother to two children

EXERCISE 19: LEARNING TO PRACTISE SELF-COMPASSION

The practice of self-compassion is allowing space for your feelings to be seen, acknowledging them, and being loving and kind to yourself whatever you are feeling. If this is difficult to do, stop, let the idea of it sink in and come to it another day.

- Sit quietly in a chair, or lie down. Connect with your feelings, observe those feelings.
- Now put your left hand on your heart. Say the following affirmations to yourself:

'I accept and allow all my feelings to be.'

'I know that I did all I could to birth my baby.'

'Thank you.'

'I love you.'

Follow this with this practice of loving-kindness from Sharon Salzberg:

May I be free from danger.
May I have mental happiness.
May I have physical happiness.
May I have ease of wellbeing.

Summary

Allow your body time to heal, especially if you have had a Caesarean birth. You may not be ill, but your body has done something powerful and amazing and it needs time to recover. Give yourself the space to appreciate that and be kind to your body, allowing it to gently come back to itself. Make use of the visualisations as an opportunity to play an active role in your own healing and to heal your body from the inside out. Allow your mind to heal, getting professional help if you feel that it would help you to process your baby's birth.

8

Thoughts and Feelings

Emotions are at the heart of becoming a
conscious mother. You cannot move from
being pregnant to not being pregnant,
without emotion.

Feeling teary in those first few days after birth can be
completely normal. Tears are not always negative; they
can be an expression of the emotional extremes of those
early days and they can happen anywhere, at any time.

Everything is responsive; not only are you responsive to
your baby, but you are also responsive to the environment
around you, and within you. The term 'baby blues' is used
very often but a friend of mine told me how she felt that term
was misleading. You may find that tears have fallen at happy
occasions like weddings, as a response to the intensity of
emotion in that moment.

Heart-opening tears

Have you thought about calling them something different,
like heart-opening tears? The opening of your heart that you
experience as a mother may feel uncomfortable and
unfamiliar; it may make you feel vulnerable as the heart is a

tender space. The tears may be puzzling; 'I don't feel sad, why am I crying?' Motherhood is about being able to have courage of the heart while still allowing tenderness and vulnerability to sit there. **PRESS PAUSE**.

'I connect with my heart, allowing all my emotions expression.'

Sometimes when we change the language around a physical expression of emotion it can change our experience. Allowing those tears to fall, without judgement or even trying to stop them, can be a healthy response to your growing sensitivity to feeling. This is important as it means that you're learning to automatically regulate your emotions in a healthy way, but also to develop capacity for you to hold your baby's emotions, as they learn how to respond to the world around them with compassion and empathy. Many women find that crying comes more easily after having children; I do! It's as if motherhood has turned up the volume on all the feels.

Tip: *Next time you feel teary at a film or when reading something, don't hold the tears in; let them flow and notice the feelings around that. Do you feel self-conscious or do you feel as if you can comfortably let it all out? If you feel self-conscious, that's your cultural upbringing. If you can comfortably let it all out, you are allowing your heart a voice.*

Riding the highs and the lows

Those early weeks can be a rollercoaster of feelings. You may go from feeling on a complete high one day to the next feeling a slump; some people call it a hump day. I call this feeling 'slumpish'. This may be something you have experienced before in life, or it may be the first time that you have experienced this. Many people have low moods, without it being a clinical problem, but what do you do on the days when you are feeling slumpish? Do you grab a box set, and a blanket, and curl up on the sofa with baby? Or do you go out for a walk with baby? Know your own remedy for these moments.

Think of your state of mind like the weather. It won't always be sunny; there will be windy days and rainy days. What is important is how you respond to the weather. I never check the weather forecast, because I know that when it rains, it rains. There is nothing I can do to change that; I adapt to it when it happens. The rain will pass, and the sun will emerge again.

> Before getting pregnant with our third child I'd had a very upsetting missed miscarriage. It had taken a while to recover physically and mentally, but finally I felt back to normal and was really excited to get pregnant again. I really enjoyed bonding with the baby during pregnancy, and felt blessed to be having a third child. The moment our baby was born though, before I'd even seen him, I had the strong feeling that this was someone different from the baby I'd been expecting. I suddenly realised I'd been waiting to see the baby that hadn't made it, and in that moment I knew I was never going to meet that lost

baby. For several weeks I felt that our newborn was a stranger – I can remember holding him in our kitchen and saying out loud: 'I don't know who you are!' I also felt joy, pride, contentment and elation in that time, but they co-existed with this sense of strangeness and an underlying sadness. I was pretty sure that our son would be our last baby, and I felt so sad about this and the idea that our family had someone missing. Some days, when the rest of the family were at work or school and it was just me and the baby in the house, I would spend most of the day in floods of tears. I was worried that I was becoming depressed, and though I knew that bonding could take time and would happen, I felt sad and guilty that I was struggling to accept my baby for being himself and couldn't just enjoy this time that I'd waited so long for. Thank goodness I'd spent the pregnancy practising mindfulness, and basically digging a well of acceptance that I could now draw from. My sensible and kind health visitor suggested I mark my bad days on the calendar so that we could track if things were getting worse. This was such a simple thing but it really helped me see that the bad days came and went like stormy weather rolling across the sky. That helped me to accept these days and get through them as best I could with as much self-compassion as I could find, knowing that another day would feel different. I drew from that well to accept my baby, accept myself and my reactions, and accept this strange time that had turned out quite differently from how I'd imagined it. I spent as much time as possible skin-to-skin or carrying my baby son, which helped me to get to know him and gradually to fall completely and besottedly in love with him. By the time he was four months old I felt very connected to him and my mood was stable again.

Jane, mother to three children

'I allow myself to let go of everything today, so I can ride this out in the best way I know.'

EXERCISE 20: YOUR SLUMPISH REMEDY

For this exercise you will need some small pieces of paper that you can write on, and a container like a small glass jar.

> **Tip:** *If you want to push this up a notch, go for it and design a big sparkly jar of happiness, covered in stickers.*

Think about the things that make you feel better, ideally those that are free and are quick and easy to do. Keep it simple, really simple, and make sure that they are things you can do with baby. Here are some ideas:

- Get fresh air and do a mindful walk.
- Do your **Calm Breath.**
- Just for today, I'm saying no.
- Listen to your **Confident Mamma** MP3.
- Put on some loud music and dance.
- Curl up with a box set.
- Order in your favourite food.

- Call a friend.
- … get creative and write your own.

Write your ideas on a piece of paper. Fold them up and put them in the jar. If you are having a slumpish day, just take one out and do it! And remember to pop it back in the jar when you are finished, ready for another day, if needed.

> **Tip:** *Read the chapter Tough Days (see page 209) for more quick mood-boosters.*

Getting motivated on a slumpish day

On days like this, it can be hard to motivate yourself. If you have things to do and are feeling unmotivated, a quick hypnosis mini-goal visualisation can help:

All you have to do is close your eyes and rehearse how you are going to do the task in your mind. Even if it's getting out to post a letter. Sit down and, in your mind, run through everything you need to do. Imagine yourself doing it. Imagine the task finished and how good it feels when that task is done. This mini-motivation tool is brilliant for all sorts of things that will happen in life, whether booking appointments, going shopping, writing forms, even emptying the nappy bin!

'If all I do today is breathe, and be, that's ok.'

There may be many reasons you may be feeling this way. Sometimes think about whether you need to fill the space.

There are days when all you need may just be acceptance that this is how it is today. Sit with those feelings without judgement, irritation or impatience. The feelings you are experiencing are just visitors today. Taking it moment by moment, accept that feeling low on energy, unmotivated or simply down is how it is. In these moments, a simple breathing exercise, like Breathe–Baby–Connect from page 97, can help to clear some space for you.

The mother's mask

Sometimes the slumps become more frequent and harder to get out of. If this is happening, are you using the mother's mask? The face you put on when you want everyone to think you are okay. Many mothers have one of these tucked away, and if you feel you are getting this out regularly ask yourself why this is. Who are you wearing it for?

I often see new mothers presenting themselves to the world as if nothing has changed. Even to the midwife, health visitor and close family. I myself remember throwing on the most cheerful smile I could muster when my midwife came to visit. It's important to allow these people to see what is real. This way it's easier for people to help and to give you the support you need.

It is normal to feel tired, to feel teary and to feel challenged, but we also have to consider postnatal depression (see also page 120). If you really don't feel as if you are coping, make an appointment to talk to your doctor or health visitor; they may come to your home if you are struggling to get out. While the words in these pages may help you reduce the stress that can contribute to your mental wellbeing after birth, I encourage you to seek out further help if this resonates with you. Sometimes the best coping mechanism is to reach out for the help that is waiting for you and baby.

I wish I could go back and talk to myself then and be told that the other mothers probably, especially the 'supermothers', weren't doing it better than me. They probably were filling all the space with their own and little ones' achievements to mask the fact that they had the same struggles that I did, perhaps even worse. I was so open and honest when I was asked at our get-togethers how I was (I was the first to have a second): I said how I felt, how it was exhausting, that I felt like I was rubbish, that it didn't come as naturally as it seemed to for others, and that I just wanted to sleep. Two of those mothers who had talked about how fantastic it was all the time told me that they had actually really struggled and daren't speak up. My honesty became a point that people could open up to – so be open, speak to your partner, your friends. You don't have to be a superhero and it's okay for it to be difficult; you have grown, birthed and are now caring for another human, who came without a manual.

Katrina, mother to two children

Postnatal Depression (PND) and Postnatal Anxiety (PNA)

Around 1 in 10 women experience postnatal depression (PND) or postnatal anxiety (PNA). There are specific risk factors, and as this is a very well-researched area of maternal wellbeing, we now know more about it than ever before. Knowing if you are at risk means that you can take steps to help get the support you need early on. You may be at higher risk if you have:

- A personal or family history of mental illness.
- A lack of social support.
- Experienced domestic abuse (emotional and/or physical).
- Financial pressures.
- Experienced stressful events in the last year.
- Had a difficult birth.

Many women do not seek help, largely because of the old stigma of mental health, or the feeling of failure that is particularly hard for new mothers.

However, becoming a new mother can be tough, and sometimes help is needed. It's important that you know it's okay to get help. If you had a physical issue you would go to your doctor, wouldn't you? Your mental health is just as important. Just because you can't see it, doesn't mean that it doesn't matter.

If you are in doubt contact your GP, midwife or other healthcare provider, or talk to your partner or a good friend. Being heard is halfway there. Think about the people you will be comfortable speaking to, and feel safe speaking to. This little exercise can help you identity the people you feel safe with. And why not do this exercise even if you don't think you have PND or PNA? It can be good to have those people and their numbers on hand if you ever feel you need to contact someone.

EXERCISE 21: WHO DO YOU FEEL SAFE WITH?

Think about where you are safe and who you feel safe with. Take a moment to pause, and really think about the people you can open up to and be honest with.

It may be your midwife, your health visitor, it may be a friend, a family member, or it may even be a group online that you feel supported by. If you can only think of one person, that's fine. If you can't think of anyone, put your healthcare provider down. Write a contact number for each person next to them. You may not need them now, but you can always look back on this chapter and use the information here to guide you.

1.

2.

3.

Looking after yourself

It's even more important to prioritise things like rest and sleep in the early days. Recent studies suggest that finding ways to manage fatigue may help to prevent the development of depression. I know this may feel like an impossible thing to do with a new baby, but resting will enable your brain to focus its energy on the physical changes that are happening in the different parts of your brain. If you are already vulnerable to mental illness, slow down and make rest a priority. Rest is a way of gently taking the pressure off your brain so it can make the changes it needs to without becoming overwhelmed. You can find creative ways to do this in the chapter on rest and sleep (see page 170).

> 'I allow myself to focus on my needs and what is important to me.'

Reduce any stress in these early days, weeks and months, whether that's unwanted visitors or balancing a household. Only do what is absolutely necessary in the first weeks.

Prioritising rest and sleep, above housework for example, will help give your body and your mind the space they need to adjust. When you do this, you are not 'doing nothing'; you are being everything you need for your wellbeing in this moment. You are taking very good care of yourself and your baby.

HOW TO GROUND YOURSELF

If you are experiencing what you think is depression or anxiety, or you have had a diagnosis, you can use grounding techniques to help in moments when you feel your thoughts running away like an express train, or you feel disconnected and spaced out. A simple one to use is connecting to the world around you through your senses. When your mind is focused on one real and present thing, it brings you back to the moment and helps you to re-centre yourself.

Think of your mind like a spotlight. While your mind is incredible and complex, and consciously able to juggle many things, you can really only focus on one thing at any one time.

Try this: Tap your fingers to the count of five, while counting the number of times the word 'your' is written on this page. It might be quite difficult to do, because your mind has to switch between the task of tapping and counting. It's just a quick reminder of how we just need to do one thing at a time.

Grounding helps you to come back to one moment, to place your spotlight on one thing. This gives your mind permission to just let go and breathe.

EXERCISE 22: SENSORY SPOTLIGHT

Your mind is like a spotlight; it can only focus on one thing at any one time. When you feel anxious or your thoughts are running away with you, your spotlight can feel as if it's moving at 100 miles an hour to try to keep up. In this exercise you use your senses to ground yourself and take control of your spotlight.

Sit or stand where you are. If you can, go outside into a garden or space where you feel safe. Wherever you are, try to keep your feet flat on the ground so you are connected with the earth. If you prefer lying flat that's okay too. Use your **Calm Breath** and take a deep breath in. 3 … 2 … 1 …, and out, relax … relax … relax …

Have a very simple mantra that you can use. Say to yourself: 'Breathing in, breathing out.' This is the centre that you come back to. If at any point your thoughts are wandering, return to your breath, and repeat in your mind: 'Breathing in, breathing out' until you feel your breath deepen. Then start the grounding exercise again.

Here is another simple technique:

1. Name three things you can see: 'I can see … ' As each thing comes into your mind, think about and then let it go.
2. Then name three things you can feel: 'I can feel … '
3. Then name three things you can hear: 'I can hear … '
4. Do this technique again on a loop if you want to keep going. If it's easier, you can do it without counting. Just allow what comes into your awareness in each moment, whether it's a bird, a car, a rumble in your tummy, your feet on the floor … Notice all of it, name it, and let it go.
5. Think about your other senses too: What can you smell or taste? Be aware of anything sensory that comes into your awareness during this exercise.
6. If your thoughts wander, pull them back to your **Calm Breath**: 'Breathing in, 3 … 2 … 1 …, breathing out, relax … relax … relax … '.

ALLOW YOUR BREATH TO HELP YOU

Understanding how you are breathing can help you to slow things down and become calmer. If you are in a state of anxiety, you are more likely to take thoracic breaths (in your upper chest) rather than diaphragmatic breaths (belly breaths).

Pause for a moment where you are and let's go over the belly breath = calm breath from Part 1. Put one hand on your chest and one hand on your belly. Close your eyes and just notice your breathing as you are. Notice the rise and fall of your hands, your breath, and notice which hand is moving more than the other. If your upper hand is moving, focus on switching your breath to your **Calm Breath** for just a few minutes. Keeping your hand on your belly, notice how your breathing begins to change, moving it down into your belly. Notice how you feel.

Whether it's for 10 seconds, one minute or longer, the **Calm Breath** encourages a lengthening breath. Learning ways to slow your breathing down can help you calm your mind and your body, at times when you feel as if your thoughts and heart are racing.

> **Tip:** *If you need visualisations to help with this, you can use the dandelion one (see page 50), gently blowing bubbles, or trying to blow and catch a feather on your breath.*

These slower, longer breaths will help trigger your soothing system. The more you practise the **Calm Breath**, the quicker your body will respond and relax.

If you feel more anxious or panicky trying this, stop, and try again in a few days. Very occasionally, people may feel panicked when they have to focus on their breathing. This just means that you may need to practise it until you feel comfortable with the action of breathing this way, and of paying attention to your breathing.

> **Tip:** *Practise this breathing when you are doing the washing up, when you go to the loo, when you are waiting for the kettle to boil or filling your car up with fuel. Anywhere that you are waiting. You could also practise it just as you are falling asleep in bed.*

LET YOUR BABY BE YOUR TEACHER

If you want to learn what diaphragmatic breathing looks like, watch your baby's belly. Babies are adept at belly breathing! Just watch your baby's breath and be aware of your own. Baby might be breathing faster than you, and that's normal and okay. They also breathe irregularly sometimes and that's normal too. The rise and fall of your baby's belly is a message to you that they are okay; they are free of worry and stress in that moment. All is well. You are doing a good job, your baby is well and resting, needing nothing in this moment. Continue to watch baby, relax your shoulders, breathe in through your nose deeply, and then out through your mouth, making a soft whooshing, sighing sound. Keep doing this for a few minutes. A few minutes is all it takes to reset your breathing and your mind.

EXERCISE 23: LADDER BREATH FOR ANXIETY

Some anxiety is 'adaptive', which means that it can be a normal response to becoming a mother; being on alert helps you to keep your baby safe. However, being able to identify what is creating heightened anxiety, and having techniques that can help to reduce that anxiety in moments when it feels overwhelming, can really help.

A 'ladder breath' is particularly good at helping in moments when you feel anxious. It may also be a better technique if you feel yourself getting anxious just focusing on breath alone. It helps you identify how you are breathing, and helps you gain control over your breath. Sometimes anxiety can feel like you are in a hole that is closing in, so let's imagine the ladder as a way of climbing out of this.

'My breath will guide me to a place of calm within me.'

Focusing on numbers and having a structure is something that many people find much better than just focusing on the breath alone:

Breathe in to the count of 1. Exhale slowly to the count of 1 (pause).
Breathe in to the count of 2. Exhale slowly to the count of 2 (pause).
Breathe in to the count of 3. Exhale slowly to the count of 3 (pause).
Breathe in to the count of 4. Exhale slowly to the count of 4 (pause).
Breathe in to the count of 5. Exhale slowly to the count of 5 (pause).

Start at the beginning again if you need to, or you can increase the numbers as you become more practised.

Ladder breath

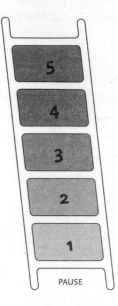

My partner seems out of character

Over the last few years we have seen an amazing shift in partners getting involved more with the parenting journey, from before birth through to getting involved in baby's care. What a difference that can make.

Part of this has been partners also becoming more aware of their own thoughts and feelings, as they grow into their role. For many years, depression or anxiety in birth partners was completely overlooked. Whether a biological partner, an adoptive father or a same-sex parent, the feelings associated with depression and anxiety can also be experienced, and for many different reasons.

Your partner will also go through changes as they transition into parenting. While studies have begun to look more closely at the maternal brain, research on the partner's brain still lags behind. Most studies have been done on male partners, fathers. We know from these studies that hormonal changes occur in them too; testosterone drops, which may make your partner more sensitive to the cues of your baby and increase affection. This has many biological advantages. Male partners also experience an increase in the hormone vasopressin, which is associated with protecting. As the brain changes, it can mean that your partner may also be vulnerable to aspects of postnatal depression, trauma and anxiety.

Other studies show oxytocin rises in everyone who is connected with caring for the baby, such as fathers and same-sex parents. When your partner is affectionate with your baby it triggers oxytocin in all of you, increasing resilience, and helping your body to learn how to manage stress more efficiently.

Summary

If you are finding it hard to lift yourself out of a slump, you are worried about yourself, or others are worried about you, the help is there for you. Contact your healthcare provider or explore the further resources in the back of this book. Use the Slumpish Remedy exercise (see page 117) to get over the days when you need a lift. If you are feeling anxious or disconnected use the Sensory Spotlight grounding exercise (see page 123). Use the ladder breath to help you climb out of the anxiety you feel in that moment.

part three

Caring for You, Caring for your Baby

9

Getting Up, Out and About

As you start to walk out on the way, the
way appears.

Rumi

After your baby is born you may want to allow yourself
time. Time to rest, time to recover, time to connect
with your baby, time to adjust with your partner, time to
allow your little family unit to bond. At some point, and that
moment is up to you, it is time to get up and leave your nest.

Although movement can be slow, it can be meaningful in
those early days.

'I connect with my body and how it feels as I
move.'

How much movement you feel comfortable with may
depend on your baby's birth. If you have had a Caesarean
birth you may need to take things more gently for the first six
weeks. If you have had a vaginal birth with no interventions,
you may want to get up and about sooner. Even then, slowing
down can be beneficial.

Notice how, at first, you handle your newborn baby with
absolute care and delicacy. Quite soon you are more confident in your movements when moving about, changing a
nappy, switching babygros; it gets easier. It will feel like

second nature before long, and you will feel really confident in handling your baby.

Each movement that you have made since your baby has been born, you have been learning about them and they have been learning about you. Connecting mindfully with that process not only helps you to slow down and notice your baby, but also helps you to realise how extraordinarily well you are adapting to being a mother.

> 'I have learned so much and am adapting at my own pace.'

Before you rush around, pay attention to your and your baby's movements. Notice the physical feelings of that movement. Observe your baby and compare the movements your baby made in the womb to the movements they are making as they begin their life outside the womb. **PRESS PAUSE**.

Fifteen days to slow down

There is a saying – 'Five days in the bed, five days on the bed, and five days around the bed' – that people have said for generations about the time after birth. It is a reminder of how important it is to slow down after birth.

Reflect on what your body has done during pregnancy and birth and you can see the value of this, can't you? Five days in bed doesn't mean you are confined to bed; do get up and take a shower etc.! But your bed is where you are able to stay and nest: you can be cosy, warm, dozing, feeding, getting to know baby. It is likely that your partner will be on parental leave, so you can snuggle up together with your baby, both bonding and connecting. If you have other children they can snuggle in too, enjoying all that oxytocin. Siblings are often fascinated by a newborn and this can be a time for them to slow down and bond with their siblings as well.

'What is my body telling me today?'

Five days on the bed is the time when you begin to emerge from the post-birth haze, but still in the fourth trimester fog. Movement may be more comfortable and you may be ready to make the bed. Or not!

Five days around the bed is as you build confidence in moving with your baby. You may be becoming more responsive to them, more aware of their feeding cues, and quicker to react as your maternal brain learns the ropes. Your body is still recovering, and gentle movement may help or it may make you more aware of what needs more healing time.

Some people may enjoy and need to be outside; it can depend on what time of year your baby is born. My summer baby allowed us to lie outside under a tree in the shade in those very early days, but with my winter baby I was very happy hibernating!

In those early weeks baby will feel comforted being close to you.

> Baby-wearing was a lifesaver for us. It allowed us to soothe our colicky baby and get s**t done!
>
> *Kym, mother to one child*

Mindful movement

You can really get to know your postnatal body through mindful movement. Your body and its movement may feel very different after birth and each day there will be changes as your body adapts. You may find that you miss your bump, or you may be enjoying feeling more like your old self.

> 'Today I will go slow and notice how my body is adapting and changing.'

Gentle, mindful movement can be done simply walking around the home at first. It encourages you to slow down and connect with your body, get to where you need to be, while also resting your mind.

Tip: *If you still have a birthing ball, and it is comfortable to sit on, why not bounce gently. Try it with baby in your arms, and as you bounce gently, notice the difference in how it feels from when baby was in your belly*

EXERCISE 24: BODY BREATHING

I love this exercise as it's so gentle and just focuses on your breathing. You can do it when you are baby-wearing or if your baby is nearby. Unlike your Calm Breath, which is a lengthening breath, this is a steady, even breath in and out.

Pay attention to the weight of your arms. With your palms facing down, raise your arms to shoulder height, and breathe in. As you move them down, slowly breathe out. Imagine that there is an even flow of breath, and your arms are softly rising and falling in time with the soft in and out of your breath. Keep your palms face down towards the floor, and let your hands be soft and gentle as you lift them and lower them.

As you breathe in, count to five slowly, and as you breathe out, count to five again. The movement of your arms should mirror your breathing. Repeat five times.

Body breathing

Breathe in

up

Breathe out

down

Confidently stepping out of your nest

As you and baby move through the fourth trimester, you may want to get out more, and this can feel like a big step! You may want to find groups to join locally, whether baby and parent groups and classes, or something just for you. There may be a wealth of choice in your area or very little. Find which groups suit you, so you can meet like-minded people. Some mothers describe it as a little like going to school for the first time, but take a deep breath and get out there. If you feel uncertain, you can use an exercise called the Bubble of Confidence and Calm to do this.

EXERCISE 25: BUBBLE OF CONFIDENCE AND CALM

Create a Bubble of Confidence and Calm in which you can be, either on your own or with baby, anywhere at any time. It can be so useful, a brilliant way to deflect things that may cause you stress. In your bubble you can learn something that I call 'casual indifference'. It doesn't mean you aren't engaged in the moment; it means that you are able to let go of things that are unhelpful.

Your Bubble of Confidence and Calm can help you do this wherever you are. When I use it, I imagine that I am Violet from *The Incredibles*, a Disney Pixar Film; her super skill is to throw a huge force field around herself and the people she loves when she feels threatened. You can imagine doing this yourself, and that a force field or bubble is around you, or you and your baby or your whole family.

Use your **Calm Breath** and close your eyes, breathing in 3 ... 2 ... 1 ..., breathing out, relax ... relax ... relax ... Imagine a colour that corresponds with what you need at that moment and breathe that colour in. As you breathe out create a strong, impenetrable bubble of confident calm around you. Imagine it like a force field. Imagine yourself in your bubble; you can move with your bubble around you, feeling calm, confident, protected and secure, wherever you go.

Your
Bubble of Confidence and Calm

Bills

Housework

Shopping

Inner
narrator

Advice

Img: Rachael Yale

Visitors

Cooking

Other
children

Demands
from others

Add your
own

....

....

....

Through having my daughter and attending NCT I have made such an amazing friend. I attribute this to going through the most incredible and vulnerable time together. It all started when we took our babies, born only a week apart, to feeding clinic. I arrived at her house in the pouring rain, terrified after making my first solo trip in the car with my newborn, and she came out with her bundle in the car seat. We realised that neither of us had any idea how to install her car seat. Naturally, we turned to YouTube, except we couldn't reach the Wi-Fi in her house and 3G/4g was down! So, my friend ran back in her house, googling frantically, and I stood in the rain praying the babies wouldn't wake up. They didn't! We learned how to install the car seat, and made it to clinic, exhausted already!! Thank goodness we learned how to install that car seat because our carpool karaoke sessions are some of my best maternity leave memories. Something felt so scary about leaving the house walking with the pram; I think that's because people might watch me and hear my baby if she cried? But in the safety of my car with my new-found bestie, we toured the Surrey Hills frequenting supermarkets and garages to give us breastfeeding fuel, singing Disney at optimum volume, so as not to wake the babies but still hit the high notes! Through this relationship I made, we have been together fighting our mother-hood demons. Attending our first playgroup, using slings and baby carriers, going for walks in the park, beginning weaning, getting through sleep depriv-ation, changing relationships, and even having the occasional mums' night out! It is a vulnerable time becoming a parent, but sometimes that vulnerability can provide opportunities for the most beautiful things to flourish. They say it takes a village to raise a child; find your village.

Sarah, mother to one child

Tip: *Use your mini-goal visualisation to rehearse going out to a new group. Imagine walking in, surrounded by your Bubble of Confidence and Calm, and being greeted by a smile, and other mums just like you.*

Sometimes the sheer volume of groups can feel overwhelming, not just for you but for baby too. You don't have to attend every group out there, and baby will not lose out from missing their musical group now and then. If you feel you would rather sit at home and have a cup of tea and chill out with baby that's fine. Your baby is going to benefit just as much from a happy, relaxed mother, content in her home.

Walking mindfully

As you get out and about, you will get the chance to do a lot of walking with your baby. You may use brisk walking as a way to re-energise yourself and this is great. But it's also good to make use of this time for 'mindful' walking. It is a very simple and easy exercise to do and can help your mind to rest, even when you are just walking to the shops.

If you can, choose to take a route through nature: past gardens, trees or through a park. Studies have shown that a walk outdoors in natural surroundings can be more restful and calming than walking along roads. If you live in a city, find a route that takes you through a park, even though it may take a little longer; it's worth it.

> I lead a local weekly 'Walking for Health' group for new and expectant parents called Bumps to Buggies. I felt that many new parents were feeling isolated and reluctant to commit to groups or classes. The walks are free, drop-in, inclusive and accessible. We get outside and gently explore nature; it's a great way to connect with yourself, your place in the world and other parents. As a midwife I could list the physical and mental benefits to walking in groups, but here are what some of the walkers say instead: 'Fulfilling', 'part of something', 'community', 'invigorating', 'energy for the rest of the day', 'friendship', 'sharing and learning', 'my own level', 'companionship'. There are a growing number of similar groups all over the country.
>
> *Jenny Parsons, midwife*

Mindful walking is slower. Rather than walking quickly to a destination, thoughts focused on what you need or where you are going, a mindful walk can be with nowhere to go but within. Research shows that connection with nature helps release oxytocin and can switch on your soothing system. Finding ways to do this regularly can contribute to your overall wellbeing.

'I breathe in deeply, exhale and smile. With each step I take I connect with the ground beneath my feet and the sky above my head.'

When you pay attention to different aspects of the walk, you benefit in a multitude of ways. Your breathing and your heart rate lowers, your mind quietens, and you are also benefiting from gentle movement.

> Without my walking group I would have found motherhood so much harder. I think it could have been quite isolating and I would not have discovered and learned anywhere near as much as I have by getting out there and socialising at baby groups.
>
> *Becky, mother to one child*

EXERCISE 26: HOW TO BE A MINDFUL WALKER

You can do this with your baby, or you can ask your partner to watch your baby while you take 10–15 minutes on your own. You could try this when you walk to the shops or to a friend's house, or just when you want to get outside.

Start with both feet on the ground and notice where you are standing. Breathe in deeply and exhale. Say to yourself: 'Breathing in and breathing out.' As you walk, notice the movement of your foot as it lifts off the ground and reconnects with the ground. Pay attention to the movement of your hips, and to your knees as they rise and fall. Notice the feelings in your body as you move. Observe any changes, what feels comfortable, or what does not. Notice what you can see, feel, hear and smell. A leaf, a flower, a car driving past. Allow your attention to name what you notice in each moment. Feelings may arise, or you may become aware of sensations in your body; notice them, name them and allow them to walk on by. If you feel your thoughts drifting, bring yourself back with this mantra in time with your walk:

'Breathing in and breathing out.'

Continue until you return to your front door, or reach your destination.

> **Tip:** *If you are short on time you can do just a 3-minute mindful walk outside with baby in your arms. Just walking a circle, perhaps in your garden. This is a great grounding exercise if you are feeling overwhelmed.*

I have found the walks have really helped me, especially months ago when I was a new mum as I just wanted to stay in, in the safety of my own home with a new precious baby. But knowing you are with other mums and a midwife who can help you in any way, it gave a lot of reassurance. Also, I think with the group being about walking it can take your mind off the baby a little, as usually most babies like the stimulation so it is a stress-free experience.

Charlotte, mother to one child

When baby wants to get on the move

When baby starts to move, it is exciting but it can be nerve-wracking at the same time! Is baby crawling or walking at the right time, are they meeting their milestones? Movement is such a big milestone to reach. Then when they do reach that milestone, how can you keep them safe and get everything out of the way? Everything, and I mean everything, will look interesting to a young child exploring the world.

'I am comfortable with you discovering your environment.'

Although you would never put soil in your mouth now, if I were to ask you to close your eyes and imagine the taste of soil, I expect you can imagine it, can't you? This means at some point you will have put soil in your mouth!

If you find yourself worrying about things like this, know that your baby will not be the first, or the last, to hoover up stale cereal off the kitchen floor, find a year-old crisp down the back of a sofa, or stuff the dog's toy in their mouth. If you have other children, it's inevitable that your baby will find things to pick up and explore. New research shows that this is an important aspect of gut population! The bacteria your baby is ingesting is helping to build their immunity to the world around them.

> **Tip:** *If you are breastfeeding, notice how your baby wants to put their hands and fingers in your mouth when they are feeding. They have been touching everything, but before you think 'yuk!' consider that what is actually happening is that they are introducing their environment to your gut, so the breastmilk you produce is perfectly tuned to build up immunity to their environment. Isn't that incredible!*

If baby is exploring, stay calm. You do need to keep your home 'clean enough' and, with other children, 'free enough' of small bits of Lego or marbles that might be choking hazards, but don't think that your home has to be immaculate at all times.

Jump into your baby's mind and look at the world from their eyes. Suddenly, their world is wider, there is a giant adventure playground on their doorstep, and they don't need you to help them explore it, they can do this on their own! It's all very exciting for them.

EXERCISE 27: EMBRACE EMPATHY

At each stage that your baby's world grows, step into their shoes for a moment with this exercise. Whether your baby is having tummy time, rolling, sitting, crawling, bum-shuffling, cruising or walking, take a moment to see the world from their perspective. I love this exercise as it is a way to be playful and connect with your own inner child. Seeing things from a different view, whatever you are doing, is a way to refresh the mind.

1.   Get down to your baby's level, and instead of playing with your baby, just be in their space.
2.   Imagine that you are looking through the curious eyes of your baby, who feels safe, secure and fearless.
3.   Notice what you can see for the first time. Where do you want to go? What looks interesting? Why?
4.   Notice what you can see, feel, hear, smell and taste!

> 'I am glad that you are exploring the world around you.'

As your baby grows and starts to walk, they will take you on mindful walks! Toddlers love to pick up every leaf, every stone, and to explore every puddle – it will take as long as it takes so why not enjoy each moment and allow them to lead. If you feel yourself wanting to hurry or that voice in your head saying, 'Come on ...', take a deep breath and name that feeling. Sometimes the feeling will be 'bored', 'impatient', 'busy'. That's a normal thought process as you, like many other people in today's society, are on go-fast.

Let your baby guide you and open your heart to the world with the curiosity of a child.

Summary

Take as long as you need to leave your nest. There is no hurry; the world is ready for you when you are ready. Connect with your body and what your body needs, as it begins to adapt and change post-birth. You'll know when you are ready to leave the nest, ready for the next stage in your journey as a mother. Use your mindful walking, and every now and again, when you are restless, change your perspective to see things differently and give yourself permission to slow down.

10

Crying

Together we will cry and face fear and grief. I will
want to take away your pain, but instead I will sit
with you and teach you how to feel it.

Brené Brown, *Daring Greatly*

One of the hardest things is the sound of your baby crying. Why are they crying? What do they want? Why won't they stop? Crying is an expression of a feeling or need. They may be too hot, too cold, hungry, in need of comfort, or the light may be too bright. There may be many things that are unsettling for your baby and while you can learn to read some cues early on, like hunger, other cues may not be so easy to read. Sometimes baby will arch away from you, and this can be very upsetting. Baby is not rejecting you; they are simply struggling with an uncomfortable feeling.

'I will comfort you and will do what I can
to provide you with what you need in this
moment.'

Sometimes you just won't know what they need and that's okay. Your brain is amazing though, and learns quickly. In fact, even in the days after your baby is born, studies show that you will have been able to pick out your baby's cry from a room full of other babies crying, with incredible accuracy.

After the first 6–8 weeks your baby's crying may start to lessen, as they adapt to their environment. They may be able to begin to communicate with simple movements and expressions. When you pay attention, and as your confidence grows, you are more able to read their cues intuitively.

'Baby, I hear you are uncomfortable, I am here for you.'

This chapter isn't about teaching you to interpret your baby's cues; you will learn how to do this when you are open to that happening, without you even thinking about it. Instead, this chapter is about getting in touch with *your* feelings when your baby is crying. You can learn how you can use techniques to help connect with yourself, and to feel calmer, which will help you to care confidently for baby in these moments, while also caring for yourself.

Meeting your baby's needs even before they get distressed is known as 'responsive care'. It helps shape a calmer brain in your baby. If your baby is scared or stressed and their parent picks them up, holds them and comforts them, they will learn about feeling comforted, which then evolves into the ability to self-comfort.

However responsive you are, there will still be times when your baby will cry. Always remember that each moment that you, or another familiar person, holds them is soothing them, even if they continue to cry. It is laying down positive pathways in their brain and teaching them how to self-regulate (the ability to respond and manage their own emotions and feelings). This is a life skill, and can mean that they will be able to calm themselves down, or cheer themselves up if they are in a slump, as a teen or adult!

You will learn that you can't always fix what your baby is feeling. This will be true throughout their life, and throughout yours as a parent. However much we want to fix things and make it better, all we can do is create a safe environment for them to explore their feelings in a secure place of comfort. This is one of the biggest lessons in acceptance as a parent. **PRESS PAUSE.**

'I feel comfortable in allowing you to find your own way to adapt to this world.'

Tip: *Use your* **Calm Breath***, and draw a figure of 8, on its side, on the palm of your hand or your baby's forehead. Time the drawing with your breathing. For a reminder of this technique, see page 49.*

Your baby will grow so quickly in the first year, and they can feel out-of-sorts each time a new feeling or emotion is thrown into the mix, just like you do. Being held and rocked sometimes isn't enough to stop crying, but by sensing your response of calm, the softness of your body as it holds them, it can help. Allow your body to soften with acceptance that the crying just is what it is in that moment. Crying is a powerful response to emotion and feeling for all humans, but especially babies.

Tip: *In these moments remember the hug from a calm heart (see page 28). Soften your shoulders and soften your body. It will feel more relaxing for both of you.*

Meeting your own feelings

In those moments when your baby is crying, what are you feeling? Do you feel capable? Do you feel calm? Do you feel confident you can meet their needs? Do you feel frustrated or angry? Do you feel confident that you are able to do all you can?

When your baby cries it can trigger a wide range of feelings, depending on how tired you are, whether you are feeling overwhelmed, whether you are hungry, whether you feel anxious or disconnected, or whether you feel calm and aware of your own feelings in that moment.

Crying is one of the most powerful triggers for difficult feelings such as frustration, sadness or anger, and it can be hard to remind yourself to stop and breathe, and to stay in the moment. It is even harder if you are tired or hungry. If you find crying triggering, for whatever reason, being able to self-regulate yourself might be something you have to learn. It can be hard to balance your own feelings with your baby's needs, and sometimes it can feel as if you are student and teacher all at the same time.

Here is an exercise to help you in these tricky moments:

EXERCISE 28: THE CALMER WAY

Use this exercise when baby is crying and you are struggling. Whether it's because you are tired, have other children to see to, or have a list of things to do, this exercise will remind you that this tricky moment will pass. It is a chance to notice what you are feeling and to let it go. You can use it as a reminder to check in with your feelings during these moments.

The CALMER way

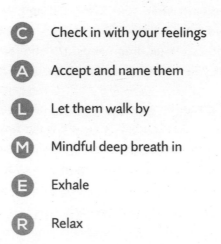

C   Check in with your feelings

A   Accept and name them

L   Let them walk by

M   Mindful deep breath in

E   Exhale

R   Relax

Listen to the **Calmer Crying** track or the **Calm Breath** when you are soothing your baby. As you focus on the words, you will calm, even as your baby continues to cry. You can play it on a loop until you feel better if you like.

Keep going, no feeling is final.

Rilke

> **Tip:** *Play music that your baby associates with being calm. If you used hypnobirthing, put on the background music of the tracks you listened to. Baby will have made the association with the music, and may remember the calm, soothing feeling of being in your womb*

Being confident that others can soothe your baby

Often, when a baby cries, the instinct of the person holding them is to pass baby back to the mother. Of course, baby is soothed by you, but your baby can also learn to self-regulate through being held lovingly by other people. Grandparents, friends and your partner can all make a difference. Research shows that if a baby is picked up, carried, or gently rocked it automatically triggers the baby's soothing system. It doesn't have to be the mother. Encourage others to help with this aspect of caring for your baby and give yourself a break. Your baby will benefit from having a mother who is rested, but will also feel soothed by the loving care of someone else.

> **Tip:** *If your baby is crying a lot, ask the person with you, whether a family member or friend, to hold baby for a little longer while you take a walk around the block or go and make (and drink!) a warm cup of tea*

My baby cries more, or less, than other babies

Sometimes babies will cry more than other babies, and sometimes less. Be guided by your instinct; if your instinct is to pick up your baby, pick them up. Some babies take a while to find their voice, to express their feelings vocally. In the early weeks after birth they will need to be held and soothed, as the world is such a new environment. Think about how you respond to disruption or shock: you may be speechless, or you might be quiet, until you feel able to find the words to express what you are feeling. The same response can happen to babies.

When my mother was pregnant with my sister, her mother died. She was just 22 and it was a traumatic and extremely stressful time. Research now shows that the extreme grief and stress my mother experienced may have impacted on my sister in utero, affecting her even after she was born. When she was born she cried every time she was put down. She needed to be soothed all the time, which was very difficult with me, her 13-month-old sister, on the scene. My mother found it very hard and went to stay with family for two weeks. During those two weeks my great-grandmother sat, and just held and soothed my sister the whole time. My mother said she hardly put her down. When she went home my sister had settled, was calmer. She cried of course, but not excessively so. This story is consistent with research; stress from pregnancy and birth can affect babies, but it can be adjusted with loving attentive care.

Sophie (me!), mother of two children

Brain plasticity (the ability of the brain to change its wiring) is amazing in young babies; you holding and caring for your baby in a loving way can create rapid changes in their calming systems.

Tip: *I have a theory: nature has a back-up plan for when parents are worn out. Who do you know that would sit, holding your baby when they are crying and you need a break? My great-grandmother was in her 80s at the time and it was a perfect match! Do you have someone in your family, or your circle of friends, who could help in this way?*

How to cope with your baby crying

I have met many mothers and parents who have struggled with crying, including some who have reached a point when they have been worried that they felt like hurting their baby. When you are exhausted yourself, and your baby is crying a lot, it can feel as if there is no end to it and no way out of it. Remember the three people you feel safe talking to from Chapter 8 (see page 121)? Can you call one of them and speak to them? Most parents have moments when they really feel overwhelmed and I am sure your three people will understand.

'I allow myself to know when I need help and I give myself permission to ask for help when I need it.'

Pin a list of jobs/things that need doing on the fridge and ask all visitors to pick one before they get to cuddle the baby. Another tip is that babies are often calmer in the mornings, so it can help to get an evening meal started then so that when the arsenic hours descend from late afternoon/early evening, when you are tired and your baby is grouchy, you can hole up on the sofa and cluster-feed, rock, pat or do whatever comforts your little person most, safe in the knowledge that you will have something nourishing to eat.

April, Antenatal Teacher

EXERCISE 29: QUICK RELEASE

This exercise helps you connect with the tension you feel in these tricky moments. By leaning into the physical tension, you are inhabiting it with awareness; allow yourself to consciously experience the tension, and then release it. Learning how to lean into those feelings without anger, moment by moment, can help you reset quicker.

'Breathe in, and let go.'

- Stand up tall and put your arms by your side.
- Breathe in deeply.
- As you breathe deeply, clench your fists tightly, as tightly as you can.
- Now as you breathe out, relax your hands.
- Let the weight of your hands pull your shoulders down.
- Roll your shoulders.
- Repeat three times.
- Then shake it out.

> **Tip:** *If you want to go deeper into this, when you breathe out make a sound deep in your throat, like deep humming. It can really help to let go vocally. Keep your jaw relaxed as you breathe out.*

Summary

Crying is baby vocalising a need. You won't always know what that need is, but they will be soothed by you holding them. As you learn to interpret their cues and they grow used to their new environment, the crying will lessen. Always remember that baby is calmed by you, but baby can also feel soothed by other familiar people, giving you a break. Ask for help, from family, friends and health professionals, if you are not coping.

11

Nourishment

I am your moon and your moonlight too
I want you to laugh, I want to
love you, to nourish you.

Rumi

With the right support and tools, feeding your baby can be a mindfully loving and emotionally rewarding experience. Think of it as an opportunity to sit down and be with your baby, experiencing that bond between the two of you. When you nourish your baby with focused attention, and connect deeply with them, your maternal brain lights up, strengthening the pathways that guide your mother's instinct.

Feeding can be a very intense experience. You may worry: 'Is my baby getting enough food? Am I doing it correctly?' This can be particularly true of breastfeeding, when stress around the correct position, or whether you are feeding your baby enough milk, can detract from the experience itself.

Knowing when to feed your baby involves a level of trust in your instincts. When you learn to look at and listen to your baby, you will become responsive to your baby's needs – your baby is amazing at telling you when they are hungry. As you tune into your baby you will learn to know when that is, and it will become a sixth sense. If you are breastfeeding, a cascade of things happen in your body and your brain that assess how much milk is needed, what type of milk, and when it's needed. This connecting and syncing is called 'limbic regulation'.

There is so much advice out there that can cloud your instincts around feeding; it can be confusing in the first few days and weeks, but it will get easier and easier. Learning when your baby is hungry is something you may feel as if you are second-guessing at first, but soon you will realise you know instinctively when they want food.

> 'I trust my instincts and I recognise when my baby is hungry.'

There is plenty of advice out there on the advantages of breastfeeding, and for good reason, and there are some great resources available that can help give you in-depth guidance. I've made a list of those at the back (see page 267). Feeding your baby is a unique journey, and one that you will experience in your own way, tuning in and responding to your baby in the best way for you.

Getting the right support for breastfeeding

You may be very well-informed on the benefits of breastfeeding; perhaps you attended classes or a group before your baby was born and learned about it then, or your midwife may have discussed it with you. The reality may be a little different; breastfeeding may happen easily for some women, while others may find it more challenging. It may be straightforward to begin with but get trickier later. Being able to confidently ask for support will help you through the more challenging times.

Good support is the key to successful breastfeeding. Historically women have always supported women with feeding and today we should be no different. Support is out there, plenty of it, and much of it free. You can optimise breast-feeding your baby by accessing support from breastfeeding support workers, breastfeeding groups, your healthcare provider and charities such as La Leche. You can also consider postnatal doulas or lactation specialists, though these are privately paid support. Not long ago I supported a woman whose confidence wavered when her baby was six months old – at *any* point in your feeding journey, help is there.

> The first few weeks I was so envious of formula-feeding mothers, and so many times nearly swapped ... by week six the pain had subsided, and I felt sorry for parents who had to get up in the night to make a bottle. Not saying one method is better than the other – just sometimes breastfeeding hurts, even if nothing is 'wrong' ... no-one had told me that, and so I spent a lot of time googling, worrying and beating myself up.
>
> *Jessika, mother to one child*

Tip: *Don't wait. If you want to breastfeed and are finding it hard going, get support as early as you can.*

Let go and go with the flow

Practical support is great but allowing yourself to go with the flow can also help. This section is about how you think and feel when it comes to feeding and how it can be another chance to create a loving bond with your baby.

When you relax during the moments you are feeding your baby, you create a space in which your connection with your baby will flourish; this is a priceless experience. Being able to relax when breastfeeding is especially important. Studies show that relaxation techniques can have a positive impact on the quality and quantity of milk produced. Your baby will feel your body soften and relax and they will sense that calm in you. Relaxation techniques (see pages 163–4) can reduce tension in your body, increasing milk flow, and improving latch.

Before you can start to use relaxation techniques, you need to allow yourself to recognise, and let go of, any worries you may have. Worry and anxiety is often fear about something that may never happen. When this philosophy is applied to feeding it's powerful. Breastfeeding can be an emotional topic, and women often, wrongly, feel guilt or failure. To breastfeed with confidence, let go of guilt, worry, fear, stress ... let go of it all.

EXERCISE 30: THE BIGGER PICTURE

When we get stressed about something we are doing or plan to do, sometimes we 'catastrophise'. This means focusing on the worst things that could happen and this can magnify stress. In this exercise I will ask you to name what you are worried about, think about the possible challenges, and ask yourself: 'How would I cope with that?' It can help you realise that you and your baby will be okay. Then the worry evaporates. When this happens, you will feel so much lighter and then it is easier to relax into feeding.

Write down here what your main concerns are around feeding:

1.

2.

3.

Now, I want you to ask yourself these questions in response to each of your concerns:

1. 'If it were to happen what are the challenges I would face?'
2. 'How would I tackle those challenges?'
3. 'What would I say to someone in that situation with the knowledge I have?'

Now let those concerns go with this simple letting go exercise:

Hold your left arm out in front of you, holding your hand closed. Imagine those concerns in the palm of your left hand. Now take a deep breath and open your hand; blow those concerns off your hand. Notice the warmth and lightness of your breath on the palm of your hand. Imagine those concerns floating away like feathers being carried away on the wind, getting smaller and smaller, until they have disappeared.

> **Tip:** *You can use this exercise for many other things. Any time you have a worry or you find yourself ruminating over something, this simple exercise helps you to stop, breathe, pause and release what has been worrying you.*

Nourishing with love

When you feed your baby and are responsive to their needs they will feel fulfilled, not just by the milk, but also by the loving connection in those moments.

'Every day I connect with my baby and I nourish my baby with love.'

I had a tough start with breastfeeding, and I think that, as well as other issues, it was down to my mind-set. I birthed a baby, using only mindful hypnobirthing, of course I was going to be able to breastfeed! That was the easy part, right? Wrong... Once I had accepted that I wasn't failing at it, that breastfeeding can be hard, it was much easier. I had issues with my milk supply, suspected tongue tie, my baby had a milk allergy and a torticollis. It felt overwhelming. So using my mind as a spotlight to bring my attention on to feeds, using 3 ... 2 ... 1..., relax ... relax ... relax ... was very helpful. We saw a cranial osteopath, I learned about galactagogues, went dairy-free, visited the breastfeeding clinic so many times, and it was tough. It can feel like you are having negative interactions with your baby when you're both learning to breastfeed, with both of you feeling frustrated trying to get the right latch and positioning. Having said all of this, I'm SO glad that I stuck with it. Leaving the house with just a change of clothes, a few nappies and my trusty boobs made things so much easier. I have carried on feeding longer than I ever thought I would. My daughter is 20 months now. Every time she has been unwell, or teething, or not sleeping I am so thankful for breastfeeding. There are days where it has been tough, and even a bit boring, but when I feel these moments, I try to remember that we are edging ever closer to our last feed, and I know I'll be so sad when that happens. I zoom in on her impossibly perfect eyelashes, and just drink her in!

My advice to any mums to be would be to seek out where you can access support for feeding before baby comes, so, find out where your clinics are, be prepared with some night-time breastfeeding snacks (my wonderful sister made me energy balls, which I kept in the freezer and would eat at 3am!), make a postnatal plan. It can feel relentless in the early days, so make sure you have support from family, friends or a postnatal doula so that you can get enough rest.

Sarah, mother to two children

Nourishing the connection

Simple hypnosis visualisations are fantastic to help you relax, and enjoy a moment of calm connection, when you are feeding your baby. These two are my favourites. They are slightly different, but I've had great feedback telling me both are very effective.

1. **Your special place**
   - This one can be used if you are bottle- or breastfeeding. When you use this while feeding, your baby will feel your body relax.

- Close your eyes and bring into your mind your special place. It may be somewhere that you have been before, that is familiar to you, or it can be completely made up. It's up to you. As you bring that place into your mind be aware of what you can see, feel and hear. Imagine it as if you are really there. Notice how your shoulders soften and relax. Enjoy this moment of relaxation and calm!

2. **The milk dial**
   - If you are breastfeeding, this visualisation is something I have given to women over the years who have had very fast flow and those who feel their flow needs a boost. I use 'dials' regularly in my hypnosis practice, as it's so easy and effective, and the more you use this technique, the easier it gets. Before you sit down, roll your shoulders back three times or do a quick stretch. Just allow your arms and chest to loosen. You can also use the Quick Release exercise (see page 155) to release tension quickly in your body.
   - Imagine a dial in your head. Give it a colour and a shape.
   - The highest setting is the strongest flow. The lowest setting is the most gentle and slow.
   - Notice where that dial is set right now.
   - Adjust the dial to where you want it to be.
   - Remember you can always adjust it while you are feeding.

Space for bonding

Where you are feeding, your environment, matters. Do you feel safe, secure and comfortable? Is everything you need within arm's length? Can you focus on baby without distraction? Think about the environment you are in and make it feel as comfortable and safe as you can. **PRESS PAUSE.**

When you feel secure, comfortable and safe, you are in a space where your connection can flourish, benefiting you and your baby with all those feel-good hormones. Whether breast- or bottle-fed, your baby can rest with you in a bubble of love, feeling nourished in body and mind.

Rest my darling
With baby's stomach full
Head tilted back into your softness
A milky smile, eyes closed
Just rest in that moment
In your baby's contentment.

Everything your baby needs is right here.
Everything you are right now is as you should be.
Rest my darling for a few moments.
And breathe.

Mindful feeding

Anyone who is feeding a baby can do this exercise; it's a chance to take a personal moment and connect with your baby. Have you noticed when your baby is feeding how they look into your eyes a lot? This is because that connection is valued; your baby is searching your face, getting to know you. Looking at your baby can build a magical connection in their brain, as well as yours. Studies show that babies of just two days old prefer faces that look back at them, and as they grow a little older brain scans show that they can process a face in more depth when it looks at them.

The time you are feeding your baby is the perfect time to spend time deepening the visual connection between you both. There will be so much change during these early days, weeks and months, and soon baby will be able to coordinate their hands, tracing the contours of your face, holding onto your finger. Often you will hear the term 'milk-drunk'; this is not just the experience of being fed, but also a result of the oxytocin that is triggered during that connection of gaze.

EXERCISE 31: FACE-TO-FACE SCAN

This simple mindfulness exercise can connect you to your baby, and help you to see your baby deeply in the moments when feeding. It means looking closely at your baby and connecting with them. It's a really lovely one to do when your baby just has a nappy on too, so you also benefit from skin-to-skin contact. If you are breastfeeding switch from right to left, or left to right depending on which side you start feeding, and if you are bottle-feeding, also switch sides.

If you are feeding on the right side:

1. Say or whisper [your baby's name]: I notice your left eyebrow, your left eyelashes, your left eye.
2. I notice your left cheek, your left ear.
3. I notice your left nostril, I notice your mouth, I notice your chin.
4. I notice your whole face, your whole face.

Switch over to the other side, and if now feeding on the left side:

1. Say or whisper [your baby's name]: I notice your right eyebrow, your right eyelashes, your right eye.

2. I notice your right cheek, I notice your right ear.
3. I notice your right nostril, your mouth, your chin.
4. I notice your whole face, your whole face.

'I am glad we have these moments together.'

Phone pledge

Can you pledge to put your phone down for at least the first five minutes of feeding your baby? It may be tempting to pick up your phone and talk to someone else, but this time is unique. It's an oxytocin-rich bubble that will benefit you and your baby. I think this is equally important with breastfed and bottle-fed babies. The pledge can be made by anyone who is feeding baby, whether partner, grandparents or siblings. Use that time to connect with baby, become aware of their face, their eyelashes, the weight of their body, the little sweat beads that sometimes form on their noses as they feed. The movement of their hands, their head. Notice it all.

Next time you feed, put your phone out of reach. Notice the feelings that arise, name them and let them go. Turn back to your baby and your breath and say to yourself: 'I breathe in patience, I breathe out restlessness.' This may be easy for you or it may be hard – if it's hard do it every now and again to train yourself to sit with those feelings as they arise, even if they are uncomfortable; be aware of them and then let them go.

By putting your phone down and being present you are giving baby something very special in those moments when both your hearts are open.

Night feeds

Getting up and down in the night can be tough, but this phase doesn't last forever. The trick to managing night feeds is getting support, resting when your baby is feeding, and knowing it will pass. Sometimes nights can be lonely and in that quiet space thoughts and feelings may have more space to be seen and heard. You can use this time to practise acceptance, to notice those feelings for what they are, and to let them go.

> **Tip:** *You can use your **Dynamic Sleep** MP3 here, or the Sensory Spotlight exercise (see page 123).*

Take each night moment by moment; surrender to the darkness, the quiet. Rest your eyes as baby is feeding; even if you aren't sleeping deeply you can rest. It all counts.

I had a text buddy in the middle of the night. If up in the night for night feeds, if needing some form of company – text another friend who is a feeding mother. Chances are you're up at the same time. Or, you can answer a text or have one answered when they're up. I actually did this for a friend six months after Maggie was born; a friend had a baby and found the night-time isolating. Maggie was a super night-feeder; therefore I didn't mind checking my phone on occasion. A few times we caught each other and had text chats about how bloody hard things were, or how cute our babies are or how lovely it can be at night – peaceful, less clutter, less busy. We would praise each other and love and feed our babies and put the world to rights. Like night secret agents growing humans and making the world a better place.

Lola, midwife and mother to two children

Summary

Make sure you get good support from your partner, family and friends, and from feeding specialists, if needed. Let go of expectation and anxiety using the techniques in this chapter to create a warm, nurturing environment for you and baby. Use the techniques to make this a peaceful, connecting and calm time with your baby. Encourage others to use the techniques if they are feeding baby as both will benefit from the loving connection that mindful feeding offers. When you are night-feeding, use the opportunity to rest your eyes; you may not notice the rest you are getting but your mind will feel the benefit.

12

Rest and Sleep

I know you're tired but come, this is the way.

Rumi

The first few months of parenting a new baby can be exhausting; there is no way to sugar-coat this. Knowing what to expect can help you to prepare and learn how to cope with the exhaustion, the best way you can. When anyone is tired, it's easier to get frustrated and angry, so learning how to adapt to this aspect of parenting can help you in every other aspect of parenting too.

While I would love to say I can make your new baby sleep and that I can create a six-hour stretch of sleep for you, I can't. But what I can offer are techniques that will help you feel more rested, and calmer. You can be tired, but not feel exhausted.

When you choose to learn techniques to help you rest, you become more able to switch on your soothing system. This can help you to optimise the surroundings for your brain and body to rest and re-energise. You can do this even when you feel as if you are getting no sleep.

'I allow my mind to rest, even when my body is awake.'

On average, new parents get less than four hours' sleep a night, yet, on average, a newborn baby sleeps 16–17 hours a day and a six-month-old sleeps 13–14 hours a day. What's going on? Why are you only getting four hours when baby is getting that much sleep? It may not feel as if your baby is sleeping 13–14 hours a day because when they are napping you may feel as if you have to get on with other things like looking after your other children, cooking, working or clearing up.

> I helped my babies get into a circadian rhythm by putting them down to sleep somewhere relatively light during the day and made it as dark as possible at night. When waking up for feeds we used a very low night light (which doesn't emit blue light) and low voices to try and keep the 'night mode'. Another thing that really helped calm my baby was playing my meditation music that I listened to out loud during pregnancy.
>
> *Liana, mother to two children*

Your need for sleep

Tiredness is not just because you aren't getting as much sleep, it's also because there is so much going on internally. Your body is healing and adapting, and your brain is reorganising to allow the perfect configuration for motherhood, building pathways between the areas in your brain that enhance empathy, responsiveness and connection. They are working hard! Be kind to yourself.

Becoming a mother is like a new job – think back to any time that you have started a new job; there was so much to learn and adapt to. Just like the early weeks and months of a new job, the early weeks and months of parenting can be tiring, even after you have settled in and you start to mother automatically.

If you think you are getting a decent amount of sleep but feel more exhausted than you think you should, this may be because you aren't getting the normal deep, restorative sleep you used to. Being able to completely switch off, even in sleep, can be a challenge because you are now your baby's protector; you are alert for them because they can't look after themselves.

EXERCISE 32: DYNAMIC SLEEP

The track **Dynamic Sleep** is a downloadable track that is just 15 minutes long. It's a guided relaxation that can help you rest and re-energise. You can listen to this sitting up, lying down and even in the bath. When baby goes to sleep it can help you switch off quickly, maximising the time you have to rest.

- Add this exercise to your self-care rainbow (see page 54) for 15 minutes of self-care.
- This track can also be listened to at night and may help you get to sleep quicker.
- You can even pop the headphones on and listen to this one if you are a passenger in a car. Use it at any time to get some rest! (Do not listen to it if you are driving or on speakers in a car.)

Be assured that if your baby needs you, you will become alert very quickly. Your unconscious is always listening out for your baby, but the beauty of hypnosis is that you can rest your mind but still be alert at a deep level.

You may want to vary listening through speakers or headphones to see which works best for you.

Mindful rest

Being constantly interruptible is a new skill that you will learn, and often it means lighter sleep as you adapt to the role of the 24/7 parent. When your baby is asleep it can be difficult to switch off from every snuffle or squeak they make; it can sometimes feel as if you are permanently on alert. Using techniques like mindfulness can help to rest your mind even when you have to be open to interruption.

EXERCISE 33: THE SNUFFLE-AND-SQUEAK MEDITATION

Whether your baby is asleep next to you, or in a Moses basket, lie near them for this meditation. Be aware of your body resting where you are lying or sitting. Be aware of where baby is resting. When they are settled, rest your eyes and rest your body. Lie on your back with your arms and legs relaxed. Focus on your breathing, breathing in a relaxed and comfortable way. Notice the coolness of your breath as you breathe in and the warmth of your breath as you breathe out. If your thoughts wander, pull them back to your breath; perhaps use: 'Breathing in I relax, breathing out I let go,' as a simple mantra. Notice what's in your environment; if you can hear your baby breathing name it 'baby breathing.' If baby snuffles, call it 'baby snuffles' and if baby squeaks, 'baby squeaks,' then come back to your own breath. If baby is quiet, notice the quiet. If feelings arise, notice your feelings, name them, let them go and then come back to your breath, breathing in and breathing out. Don't jump to your baby immediately when they make a noise; just observe that noise or movement calmly and let it go. Baby will let you know when they need picking up!

If you feel your thoughts running away with you, come back to the mantra:

'Breathing in I am calm, breathing out I let go.
Breathing in I am calm, breathing out I let go'.

Then start again to notice your baby's snuffles, squeaks and silences.

The difference between rest and sleep

When you are finding it difficult to carve out time to sleep and your sleep is interrupted, think about rest instead. This is why the time you take for the fourth trimester is so important – it lays down a foundation of rest upon which you can build the first year. Rest is powerful – even though it's not sleep it still makes an enormous difference to your wellbeing. By allowing yourself to lean into those early weeks of being with your baby at home, and doing as little as possible, you are allowing your body and mind to rest and heal by placing fewer demands on yourself. You are creating the space to notice your baby, and to notice what you need at a much deeper and more intuitive level. **PRESS PAUSE.**

'I allow myself to prioritise rest and prioritise
what is important for me and baby.'

Yes, you may want to get out and about and do things, but many mothers I speak to who have done that in the past say that they wished they had rested more with their previous babies. When they chose to hibernate and nest, they have loved being able to switch the outside world off and felt a deeper connection with themselves, their baby and their family. If you have other children, depending on their ages, there will be things that they can do to help around the home; you may find your older children surprise you and get more involved than you expected.

When my fourth baby was born, I was worried about how I would cope as my husband works long hours and my other three children were 11, 7 and 4. In fact, the children really stepped up, helping around the home more as well as with their little sister. It established really helpful routines and now they don't think twice about emptying the dishwasher. I still feel the exhaustion that any new mother feels, but my other children just worked it out.

Kate, mother to four children

Allowing yourself to sink into the upheaval of those early weeks is a powerful and wise choice. You are making an active decision to allow yourself to be in a place of acceptance. When you do that you free yourself from suffering. By this I mean the narrative of, 'I'm so tired', 'will I ever sleep again', 'this is the worst', 'I need sleep or I won't function'. This rumination can be exhausting in itself. Being mindful of your thoughts and expressing kindness towards your experience can allow a gentler experience in the moment. Treat tiredness as a guest, someone who is teaching you how deep your depths are.

Tip: *Spend one day consciously halting the 'I'm so tired' narrative, and instead replace it with something encouraging or positive and see how it feels.*

Hypnosis for rest

Hypnosis and dynamic sleep relaxations are brilliant for rest, allowing space and time for your body and brain to rest when time is limited. Research shows that just 30 minutes of a dynamic sleep exercise can be the equivalent to 2–3 hours of sleep. In a deep state of hypnosis your brain waves can slow down to 'theta' waves. This means that your brain waves are slowing down to a pace associated with relaxation and creativity and best of all, deep sleep! You typically experience this when you are daydreaming, or even when you drive somewhere familiar and get there without really thinking about it. There is a lot of current research exploring ways of accessing the potential that theta brain waves offer us – meditation and hypnosis are two ways to do this.

The benefits of hypnosis sleep relaxations include:

- Stress reduction
- Increased understanding of internal sensations
- Increased understanding of the feelings arising out of emotions
- Helping to heal your body and mind
- Helping to reduce physical and mental fatigue

Tip: *If you practise yoga, then you may be familiar with the yoga nidra exercise, which has the same benefits. You may find that yoga nidra suits you well as it will be more familiar, so this is a reminder to keep it going during these tiring nights.*

Don't tell me to sleep when my baby sleeps!

When I was a new mother I was told: 'Sleep when baby is sleeping.' Like other women I found this very difficult to do. When baby was sleeping, often it was my only opportunity to get things done or spend time with my other child. It can seem that there are a million and one things that need your attention when you have a new baby. Even though it may be frustrating to hear, there is a reason why you hear this phrase so often because it contributes to your wellbeing in the first year. If you are exhausted, sleep or rest are priorities above washing up or loading the dishwasher. If you can't sleep, explore the other ways of resting that are in this chapter.

> The old adage 'sleep when they do'; I swear it saved me. Even if it meant sleeping upright on the couch with my little one in the sling! My daughter did not sleep through the night until she was 18 months old and was waking for feeds until she was one. But I never felt exhausted or sleep-deprived because I stuck to this rule, catching catnaps whenever I could.
>
> I used a short hypnosis relaxation track to help me get off to sleep during the day so I wasn't worrying about the laundry, dishes and toys piling up around me!
>
> *Rachel, mother to one child*

If you can prioritise tasks that have to be done, and which can wait, you can create moments when you can sit quietly and shut your eyes, or do a relaxation track.

Active rest

You can also think of rest in a different way; do you believe that rest always needs to be passive? Think again! Energising, renewing rest can be active. Sometimes physical activity in which we allow our minds to rest can be invigorating and activating.

Rest doesn't have to be lying on a sofa, or in bed doing nothing. Rest can be moments in which you do something

Tip: *Use your mini-goals visualisation (see page 118) to do some rehearsal imagery around doing active rest. It may be hard to get up to do something, but if you know that you will feel better when you have done it, rehearsing it in your mind before you do it will help boost your motivation.*

that is active and which refreshes you while resting your mind. For example, many people find that fresh air and a walk can energise. This is a form of active rest.

I've put some examples here to get you started but you may want to add your own if there is something that you love to do that is active, but calms and rests your mind. When you do it think about altering the way you do it, by connecting with your breath and paying attention to where your awareness is.

- Walking meditation or just a walk with some deep breathing (see page 143).
- Mindful Shower (see below).
- Baby massage (see below).
- Gentle yoga stretches. You may want to take some classes to help you find gentle yoga exercises that are right for you at this time, especially if you have had a Caesarean birth.

Mindful shower

This is so simple. Next time you are in the shower, try this exercise. First, have gratitude for the shower. It is a small but nurturing thing; it is your self-care. I know it can feel as if you can't even get a shower sometimes, but when you do have one, do it mindfully and don't rush. Focus on your breathing and add gratitude to the moment:

> 'I get to have warm, clean, water to shower under.'

Using your **Calm Breath** to centre yourself, notice your breathing. Breathing in and breathing out. Notice the water on your skin, the sound of the water, the drops, the steam. If you are disturbed by a noise or an interruption, stay calm with your breath, and just notice the disturbance. It is what it is. Rest in that awareness. Then as you are doing each of these things use these statements:

'As I am showering, I am showering myself with care.'
'As I refresh my body, I am refreshing my mind.'
'As I am washing my hair, I am washing away fatigue.'

Baby massage

Research shows that touch is one of the most powerful ways to release oxytocin and dopamine. Studies on massage and touch are now demonstrating that patients who have received healing touch experience accelerated wound-healing, relaxation, pain relief and general comfort. Baby massage is very popular for good reason, and you can learn how to massage your baby easily. Massaging your baby mindfully can be a form of active rest for you too, and is also a great bonding exercise with baby.

EXERCISE 34: MINDFUL MASSAGE

This is soothing for your baby, and for you, and is ideal for just before bedtime. Set some time aside to do this every week or even every day; I used to do it every bedtime. Even when you are tired, this exercise will rest your mind as your attention is focused on baby and on the gentle movements of the massage.

When you massage your baby, really notice them. As you hold them, as you put them down, breathe in their smell, and breathe out any stress or worry. The smell of your baby will release serotonin, a chemical in your brain that makes you feel good. You don't have to speak as you massage them, just be with the touch. Notice how your baby's skin feels and how they respond. Be guided by your baby.

Rest your baby on a mat and smile at them. Even if you don't feel like smiling the act of doing it will release serotonin, so soon you will feel better. Notice how your baby is in this moment without judgement. Gently massage your baby's feet, legs, fingers, arms, cheeks, temples and forehead. Look into your baby's eyes and say: 'I am glad that you are here.' Notice your feelings. Acknowledge what you are feeling. Breathe in 3 … 2 … 1 …, breathe out, relax … relax … relax …

Gentle yoga poses

If you already do yoga you'll understand the benefits. If you don't, and there is a postnatal yoga class nearby, go and check it out. You can do it with baby – best of all, it's very gentle and can be restorative and energising. And it's for YOU! If you do this class, put it on your self-care rainbow (see page 54), and each time you do it you will have contributed to your self-care.

The first time I tried a mum and baby yoga class I actually cried with frustration. My baby was still only a few weeks old and I spent most of the class feeding him and changing nappies, thinking about how desperate I was to stretch my tight shoulders! But as the weeks went by the class became the highlight of my week – it was really good to be giving my tired and aching body some much-needed care and attention, and I absolutely loved doing the yoga poses with my baby. We had so much fun together, and aged six he still loves doing the 'flying baby'!

Guin, mother to three children

The curve ball

Just when you think you've got it sussed and your baby is starting to sleep for longer stretches, they will have a growth spurt. When this happens, it can feel discouraging as it's hard to understand what's happening; why has your baby suddenly started waking up through the night again? This can feel so discouraging, but this phase will pass. Growth spurts involve quite a bit of reshuffling around in your baby's brain – the brain is physically getting bigger but also neurological changes are happening at an impressive rate.

'I see that you are growing, I am growing with you.'

With brain growth comes physical growth: limbs will be growing, which can feel a bit achy, and your baby will also feel hungrier as they need to fuel this rapid growth. These spurts continue as your baby grows; we all know that teens have massive growth spurts because they can very easily (and grumpily) communicate that their joints ache and they are starving. The same is true of babies and toddlers; they just communicate differently!

If your baby's sleep pattern changes suddenly at around four or seven months, or anywhere in between, think of it not as a regression but as progression. If you feel disheartened, you can use this little hypnosis visualisation:

EXERCISE 35: THE INNER HUG

When deep tiredness hits, and with it a sense of despair that you are going backwards, all you can do is accept that this is a tough moment of being a mother. You will get through this. Tapping into your own inner strength during these times will help you quieten the narrative in your head. Use that strength to lean into the exhaustion and to put one foot in front of the other.

1. Sit down and rest your eyes. Take a deep breath in. As you breathe out let go. Let go of the tiredness. Name and let go of anything else that is hard right now. Now clench your fists as hard as you can and then relax them. Notice the tension leaving your body. Do it again, and lean into the soft tiredness of your body. Let your shoulders go soft and your belly go soft.
2. Now imagine that the part of you that knows this will pass is standing in front of you. She tells you: 'I know this is hard, and I know you are tired, I see you, I am with you. You can do this. It will pass.'
3. Imagine her giving you the biggest, warmest hug and as she does you feel all her strength moving into you. In this moment, say to yourself: 'Keep going, you can do this.'

> I say to myself, 'one hour at a time, one day at a time'. There's no need to think too far ahead, just deal with the here and now, as sometimes it can feel so overwhelming.
>
> *Julia, mother to two children*

Tip: *If you feel like crying, do! Let it go, all of it!*

Creating hypnosis anchors for sleep

It's never too early to learn a few tricks for bedtime and for getting baby to sleep in an unfamiliar space. This establishes a routine for you and baby that can feel soothing. Conditioning by association is very powerful, and I often use It In my work. It means repeating something that you can see, feel, hear, smell or taste, while experiencing a certain feeling. For example, if you were to go on holiday and hear the same song over and over again, whenever you heard that song you would immediately think of your holiday and those happy times, which can help you to relax. **PRESS PAUSE.**

I want you to think about any routines you have for sleep. Can you go to bed without brushing your teeth? Do you need to have locked the doors and closed the curtains? Think about whether you sleep well with the light on or off. These routines are part of your bedtime association.

Now just pause for a moment where you are.

Close your eyes and think about what you need in order to go to sleep. It may be something you do, something you need to have around you.

Your associations are completely unique to you and have developed over years. There are some that may still linger from your childhood, or they may have been newly developed as an adult.

Beginning to create these associations very early on for baby, in a gentle loving way, can be beneficial to you and your baby. You can build a space of calm, safety, security and familiarity around sleep. I'm going to show you how you can develop 'anchors' associated with sleep. These will become a tool that you can use to help your baby go to sleep, at home or anywhere else.

EXERCISE 36: THE SLEEPY EIGHT

You can start building this up when your baby is around six months old or when a clear bedtime routine begins to emerge. This may be around bath time, massage time, or the last feed of the day; typically, a time when your baby is drowsy and just as are you are putting them into bed at night. Do it each night if you can, so it becomes part of your routine.

Take a deep breath, smile at your baby, and put them in the bed where they sleep. Stroke the number 8 on their head slowly, and say softly: 'Breathing in 3 ... 2 ... 1 ..., breathing out relax ... relax ... relax ... '. Whatever they do, keep calmly stroking; if they are fretful, stay calm and keep doing this gently, keeping a slow, soft, even pace. If they are so fretful it's hard to do, just say it in a calming voice. Your baby won't understand the verbal instruction yet, which is why the tone of your voice and your calm presence is so important.

Sometimes life does get in the way and you may feel that you haven't got the energy or the headspace to do this every day of the week, but keep it as regular as you can. The association gets stronger each time you do it.

After around two weeks of doing this exercise, your baby will begin to associate the cadence of your voice, and the action, with feeling tired. When this happens, you can begin to take it into other situations to help settle and soothe your baby.

> **Tip:** *Try this soothing technique on yourself by tracing the number 8 on the palm of your hand. Try it when you go to bed, or want to rest, and see how it feels!*

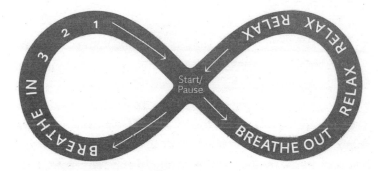

Summary

If you can't sleep, just rest instead with your baby. This can mean lying beside your baby, resting your eyes, and doing the snuffle-and-squeak meditation. Pop the **Dynamic Sleep** track on, if you need help to drop off. Look at active rest exercises to help keep your energy levels up and to help you rest your mind. Have confidence that you will feel rested again and that this aspect of parenting will get better.

13

Relationships

You can do what I cannot do. I can do what
you cannot do. Together we can do great
things.

Mother Teresa

Your baby is here, and suddenly you and your partner are tested in ways that you may not have imagined. All relationships go through phases where you have to work harder at them, and becoming parents may be one of those times. You may be familiar with the ebb and flow of all relationships; not just partners, but friends and family too. Having a baby can throw things into the spotlight and can create steep learning curves, even in the most solid of relationships – this can be normal.

You may each be processing your own feelings around becoming a parent. You will both be tired; fatigue can put anything under pressure and it can highlight flaws and disconnection. You may have different expectations or desires around parenting, but equally this is a wonderful chance to grow and develop into the parents you are becoming.

'I love that we are a team.'

Parenting together

Although you are in this together, it may not always feel this way. You are on parallel parenting journeys, sharing the adventure together but experiencing in it in different ways. This will be the same for the rest of your lives.

Your baby will look to you for different things at different times. In those early days, you, the mother, are biologically primed for your baby's needs, and your baby will look to you for nourishment and security. Over the years the 'go-to parent' will change according to your child's needs – one of you will be the go-to parent, while the other is supporting in the background doing what needs to be done to support the family.

Creating opportunities for your partner to be involved, and allowing the space for this to happen, can be the foundation for a healthy relationship and parenting partnership. Equally, studies show that the more partners are engaged early on, the more involved they become with their children's lives in the long term.

Think of things that you and your partner can do together:

- Change a nappy together.
- Choose your baby's clothes. Fold the clothes and put them away in their room.
- Bathe your baby, and get them ready for bed.
- Go for a walk.
- ....
- ....

You are both learning how to care for this little person and doing things together in those very early days will give each of you the confidence to know that the other is comfortable with what they are doing. As your confidence grows you will then both be able to take on different tasks, as and when they are needed, confident that the other knows what they are doing.

> 'I am glad that you and I are doing this together.'

In reality, you may fold the babygros differently, have a different nappy routine, or slightly different bath routine, but does that really matter? It's so much better to know that you can nip out and leave your partner with baby confidently, without having to explain where everything is or how baby likes things to be done.

> 'I have trust that our baby will adapt and learn comfortably when things are sometimes done differently.'

The secret to supporting each other in the first year, particularly in those early weeks, is to lean into each other in little ways, each and every day. Sometimes just saying: 'Shall I make a cup of tea for us?' is an offer of kindness, especially if you hold baby while they drink their tea hot!

I had an 'unexpected' pregnancy with my third baby and struggled to come to terms with it as my career was just taking off. My new husband was delighted (he thought he'd never have children). We started a weekday routine of 6 o'clock bath time. MY bath time! He got to spend an hour with his new baby all to himself. He sang to her, took her out for a walk, watched football on TV with her and rocked her when she was going through a grizzly period. Meanwhile, I made sure she'd had lots of feeds before 6pm and then relaxed in a deep bubble bath with a good book. Magic! It restored my calm and gave me precious moments on my own. Sometimes I voluntarily cut the hour short and went to spend time with the teenagers, but I knew the hour was mine if I needed it. I coped much better with the day knowing I would have some time alone at the end of it. Looking back I'm amazed it worked so well; the baby genuinely didn't seem to need me for that hour apart from the rare occasions she was ill when, of course, I abandoned my bath. My husband says he used to drive home smiling looking forward to his special hour.

Valerie, mother to three children

EXERCISE 37: KICK-START KINDNESS

Kindnesses can make such a difference. They can make you and your partner feel seen and valued. If your mind is empty and you can't think of anything, or you are feeling a bit tired and grumpy, it can be hard to think of something kind in the moment. We are going to create a list here, so that you will have something ready to choose, and then do it.

Write down five simple gestures that are personal to you and which can make a difference. They need to be simple, such as: making a sandwich, running a bath, putting your favourite playlist on, a head or foot massage, buying a favourite drink, creating a cinema date at home ... I was often too tired to change the bedding and my husband would do it while I had a shower; there was nothing nicer in those early days than sinking into fresh, dry, comfortable bedding that didn't smell of milk! It made me feel cared for too. Encouragement is a form of kindness – encourage your partner to do some of the things they may be missing, like going for a run or seeing friends too.

1.

2.

3.

4.

5.

The tiredness Olympics

Tiredness is not a competition. You will both be feeling tired, and exhaustion may give rise to feelings of frustration, resentment and stress. It may be that your partner is able to fall asleep quicker than you for the simple reason that your brain is primed to stay on alert for baby's hunger cues.

When my children were born I began to resent the fact my husband could fall asleep anywhere, at any time. In my exhaustion, I neglected to see that while I was exhausted and had a baby to care for the next day, he was also exhausted and had a job to go to. I couldn't take his tiredness away any more than he could take mine away. We could both accept it, and find ways to sit with it, being kind to each other.

Something I talk to my girlfriends about is how our relationships have changed. You are both doing your best to keep this tiny person alive but somewhere in the midst of sleep deprivation and hormones, you start talking a different language. And often you just can't understand each other any more. You have to try to be nice to each other again, make the effort, make conversation, compliment each other on your efforts and progress with your baby, explain why you are doing something a certain way. Don't get into the 'who is more tired contest'. (FYI it's me!)

Sarah, mother to one child

Tip: *It can be helpful to find ways of resting together; think back to some of the exercises on active rest (see pages 177–9). Going for a walk together, with or without your baby, can energise both of you and be connecting.*

Think about being on the same team instead of creating a narrative around who is more tired. Instead of competition, think about your strengths and play to them as a team. You don't both have to be awake at the same time, all the time, with baby. It may not be a competition, but you can be on the same relay team, although instead of a baton you have a baby. Encourage each other, hug each other, and give each other a break.

EXERCISE 38: HOW WAS YOUR DAY?

Active listening is really powerful. Studies show that relationships are stronger when partners in a relationship feel seen and heard. Both of you have to commit and be willing to do this on a regular basis. Make it a habit and this will serve you well in the years to come. My husband and I still do this every day, although sometimes he has to remind me to switch my phone off! Aim for five minutes each day. You can do this while taking baby out for a walk, or while baby is feeding, or when they have gone to bed. Think of moments that you can focus on each other even if baby is there.

- Put devices away and switch them to silent or off.
- Make a cup of tea.
- Be present with each other while you talk.
- Ask each other how their day was.
- Show you are listening by asking questions.
- If it was rubbish say: 'I'm sorry it was so tough,' and hug them.
- If it was great say: 'I am glad you had a good day,' even if your day was rubbish.

Once a week just make 15 minutes to sit and talk about how each other is, and ask about each other and anything else that might have cropped up.

Parenting confidently from the same page

It's never too early to think about parenting styles, and undoubtedly there will be experiences very early on that may surprise you about your partner's parenting style. You may have discussed parenting styles before baby was born or you may not. You may have assumed that because you get along so well, and you have similar values in other areas of your life, this would also extend to parenting. Areas that can cause conflict in the early days may be small or more challenging.

Staying calm in those moments can be challenging and your confidence may waver, especially if you trust and love your partner deeply. The ambivalence you feel may not just be feelings about your baby, but also about your partner.

You may love them but feel anger and frustration towards them at the same time.

Having differing parenting styles can be a positive thing. Slightly different approaches to parenting give children a wider view of adult values and a chance to have a unique relationship with each parent. It can also help build resilience if those differences are not a source of open conflict between parents. As long as parents come together as a united front, it can be healthy.

EXERCISE 39: RECONCILING DIFFERENCES

In this exercise we are going to look at how you can understand each other's approach to parenting. It is also a chance to think about your parenting goals. If you like, you could write this up as your family's 'parenting manifesto' and put the points somewhere you can see them. Being a co-parent is something you may need to learn to adapt to. When you prepare, and work as a team, it can help you to learn where to compromise, let go, to step in and step back. You will have differences as parents, but learning how to meet in the middle when that happens will make it easier to reconcile differences with calm clarity instead of confused conflict.

- Set a joint parenting goal: Talk about what type of child you want to raise. What type of parenting methods support this? Look into them and discuss them in relation to your own and each other's expectations.
- Research and explore your parenting styles: There is now so much research on the impact of different styles of parenting. Advances in psychology mean that more than ever we are able to understand what influences mental and physical wellbeing in our children in

the long term. We know how to build resilience and raise loving, kind and compassionate human beings. You may want to have a different approach to your own parents.

- Look at what you have in common: Think about what you have in common in terms of parenting; there might be far more than you think! For example, you both want to do what is best for your baby.
- Identify what are your strengths. This can be a positive way to look at all the things you do really well.

Sex and intimacy

Sex and intimacy can be quite a key topic for new parents. Sex and intimacy can both be very physical, but unlike sex, intimacy doesn't have to be a physical shared experience; it can also be an emotional shared experience. The physical aspects of your relationship may throw up many questions in the weeks and months after your baby's birth. When is the right time? Will it be the same as before? It is a very individual experience; some people may feel ready for sex just a few weeks after baby is born, and others may not even have it on their mind at all. Your feelings may depend on the type of birth you have had and that's okay. If you feel sore, uncomfortable or you really don't want to have sex, wait. This can be a perfectly normal response. Hormones play a part too; as prolactin increases in your body, supporting maternal behaviour and breastfeeding, it can also suppress the desire for sex.

If you are concerned that you are losing the intimacy and closeness you had by not having sex, then there are other ways to connect intimately after having a baby. Emotional intimacy can be maintained by taking simple and small steps.

The new shared experiences and communication we have already looked at in this chapter are all a form of intimacy. Being absolutely present with your partner when you are talking to them is important; when you are talking, put your phone down, and look at them.

Create opportunities to do things together, like bathing your baby. People often talk about date nights and while this can be a fantastic thing to do, it can be quite challenging to ensure this happens regularly when you have a young baby. Simple things like going for a walk, with baby happy in the sling or pushchair, can give you time to talk to each other. Getting a coffee and sitting on a park bench counts too; it doesn't have to be an evening out.

Touch is very powerful, and vital for maintaining intimacy. Why not hold hands while you are sitting on the sofa watching box sets? Sometimes just sitting on the sofa feeling exhausted together forms a bond of intimacy and togetherness.

If you both meditate already, keep going! Create your own family 'sangha'. Sangha means community. Even if you are used to longer stretches of meditation, see if you can find five or ten minutes a day that you can set aside to meditate together. If you are both interested in meditation, this is something you can start together. In the moments you are sitting, you are resting your mind while still connecting at a deep level.

Birthing my children left me with three scars, from a Caesarean, a 3rd-degree tear and lastly a 2nd-degree tear (by far the simplest stitches, expertly sutured by my midwife at home!). After each birth I felt like I wouldn't care if I never had sex again. By the time I had healed physically, I was completely immersed in the day-to-day physicality of caring for the baby and children, feeling pretty 'touched out' by the end of the day. My sex drive took months to come back, and I am so grateful to my husband for understanding and patiently accepting that my need to focus on nurturing the baby was stronger than anything else. Eventually it did return of course, and sex now is better than ever!

Guinevere, mother to three children

Tip: *Use your phone map or a paper map to look for new places to visit that are under an hour from you, and that you might not have discovered before children! Look for parks, museums, walks and events that you can do together with baby. Sharing new experiences is a great way to get out and build a feeling of intimacy.*

Why communication matters

It may be that when you are exhausted and busy with baby, frustrations are close to the surface. What you say can feel critical or supportive and inclusive. Speaking with kindness doesn't take any more time, and can make you both feel acknowledged. Here are two examples:

Don't say: 'You've put the nappy on back to front, now look what I have to sort out.'

Do say: 'It's tough learning how to do all of this isn't it. I'll fetch the nappies and let's tackle this poonami together.'

Don't say: 'You never have time for me.'

Do say: 'I really loved it when we cuddled up on the sofa the other night.'

Positive sticky notes

In many studies about successful long-term relationships, one theme has been the value of simply noticing the other person and valuing their place in, and contribution to, your world. At a time when your relationship is evolving rapidly, showing appreciation towards each other is very powerful. It builds confidence in both your abilities to parent, and also confidence in your relationship.

Take a moment to notice what your partner does. What do they do that helps you, even if it's something you think they should be doing anyway? Look at what they are doing. When you think of something kind or positive, write it on a sticky note and leave it somewhere that they can see, for example, on their pillow, or on the shower for them to see when they wake up. If something occurs to you during the day, why not send a text, if it comes into your mind? Start your note with one of these phrases if you like:

'I am glad ... '
'Thank you for .... '
'I loved it when you ... '
'I see you, I love you, I am here for you.'

Forgiveness

One of the most powerful things in any relationship, particularly when you are muddling your way through the first year of being parents, is forgiveness. Sometimes, when you are so swept up in tiredness, it can be very easy to get upset, say things you didn't mean, or say things that are mean. Showing forgiveness is a simple way to connect; this can be forgiveness towards yourself and to others. I am a big believer in apologising. In life, there is a time for standing your ground but there is also a time for accepting that you said something or did something that caused another person to feel sad. This is often not intentional and happens most during those moments of exhaustion or stress. Saying sorry is not about admitting guilt; it's about accepting what happened, stepping into the discomfort, and acknowledging your partner's feelings. Don't make excuses, don't blame the lack of sleep or anything else; it is what it is! Forgiveness should be a simple, vulnerable act, free of blame or guilt. This is where its power lies.

Even when you don't feel like saying it, the words: 'I'm sorry, I love you, please forgive me,' may surprise you in their ability to dissolve any lingering anger, frustration or hurt.

Summary

Notice the small things that both of you do, and foster opportunities for emotional intimacy with new and shared experiences. Remember that both of you are on the same, but different, parenting path. Communicate and share your feelings, forgive often, thank often and say 'I love you' a lot.

14

Cultivating Connection

I live my life in widening circles that reach out
across the world.

Rilke

Connections are one of the most important aspects of
parenting in the first year. Becoming a mother can feel
very lonely at times, and you may wonder if you are the only
person who feels this way. Rest assured you are not the first
mother to need support, shared experience and connection
in the first year (and beyond).

During pregnancy you may have begun to develop new
friendships, extending your support network through antenatal classes, making connections with others on the same
journey. You may be surrounded by family and friends
nearby and feel very well supported, or you may feel isolated
and lonely if you are living away from your support network.
As our society has grown, people have migrated away from
families, from villages to cities and across countries, towards
jobs and opportunities.

Support is one of the most important building blocks for
a confident and calm first year. Research shows that empathic
and caring support can really help you to build your confidence as a mother.

You may be extroverted and feel comfortable surround-
ing yourself with lots of people or you may be more

comfortable with fewer people around you. Pay attention to your feelings and whether you feel comfortable or not having people around you. Let's look at the three main ways of finding connections:

- Cultivating connection with your family.
- Cultivating connection with your friends. .
- Cultivating connection with your wider community.

Family

Cultivating connection with your close family can be very important in those early days. The relationship and bond your baby will have with their siblings and grandparents, for example, may be very special. However, remember to limit your visitors in the early days if you need to. Use the exercise Bubble of Confidence and Calm (see page 138) to help create a safe space.

It can be helpful to encourage family members to develop a connection with baby early on. Baby will be soothed by people who are familiar and who are loving towards them. Have a think about which family members will be great support.

Friends

You may find that friends you expected to be there aren't, and others may step up; the friendships you expected to become tighter during this phase of your life may be different to how you expected. While this can be challenging, recognising the flow of friends in and out of your life can help you to accept the nature of change in relationships. Consider how this has happened in your life. Can you:

- Think of one friend who has popped up at different stages of your life?
- Think of a friend who you haven't seen for ages but who you know you can connect with?

By focusing on this you can begin to reflect on your friendships. They aren't any less because they are transient; in fact this positive ebb and flow of relationships means there is always opportunity for people to arrive and inhabit this space in your life. Whoever is in your life in this moment may be just who you need to be there. If it's not, let them go, for now anyway.

For both Maggie and Tove, Sian and I spent hours, days, weeks preparing naming ceremonies for our daughters, both several months after birth. Sitting together and choosing an 'oddmother' was so reassuring; we felt that we had a fab 'village' to bring up our child/children. We chose eight friends for each of the girls (some of them twice) based on their extraordinary qualities they could bring to our girls and to us as parents. We asked each of the oddmothers to in turn mother us as we mother. (Now I'm getting homesick for our village of women.) Sian and I knew we had an amazing group of friends around, some parents, some not. Some in relationships, some not. Some down the road, some not. It was a valuable and enjoyable experience to 'formalise' creating a circle of friends and mothers around us, and this also helped us to realise our qualities too. Talking about and sharing your innermost gushes about the qualities you appreciate in others is so rewarding. Again, this is all part of daily gratitude. On the day of the ceremonies, the love that surrounded our daughters and us was affirming of the power of a village. I remember reading some cards out aloud to Maggie and thinking, I'll keep these cards and read them to Maggie if she is ever in doubt of herself or how deeply loved she is. If she's having a bad day – these cards will be so lovely.

Lola, mother to two children

Wider community

Communities have always been, and will continue to be, important in supporting families, although it has changed significantly in the last hundred years. More people are educated at universities, often away from their communities; there's movement to the cities for jobs; and the majority of women give birth in hospital now. This all means that we no longer experience the traditional sense of people gathering around a family or mother after birth. We have had to create new communities. There are pockets of support that you can find in postnatal groups, but you may have to be proactive. If you love getting out and about meeting new people, this may be easy for you to do, but some people find it harder socially, and it's not uncommon to feel anxious, even if you used to feel comfortable and adaptive when it came to meeting new people.

'I open my heart and mind to connection,
allowing it to happen comfortably.'

To help with this you can use a hypnosis visualisation. Think back to the section on setting mini-goals, being the director of your own script (see page 47). If you want to go to a group and are feeling anxious, rehearse it mentally: write the script and play it out in your mind. Bring other tools in, like the Bubble of Confidence and Calm (see page 138). Imagine yourself as confident, finding someone to talk to, or just being comfortable in that unfamiliar place with baby – not feeling the need to talk to anyone. You are the scriptwriter and it's up to you.

Look for clubs and venues locally that welcome families and are great communities to get involved in. Leisure centres and sports clubs, in particular, are usually family-orientated and some have cafés and facilities attached. Arts centres, church halls, playgroups, cafés and nurseries may all advertise groups you may like to try. There are lots of groups advertised online too, which can be great if you want to meet others in your area, and ideal if you want to find a group for twins and triplets, or bilingual families, for example.

> 'My baby and I are getting to know our community together.'

Going for a walk and saying hello to people you pass in the street helps to connect again. I started to get involved with mothers and toddlers and other groups to meet other parents. I think that's really important because you can find yourself detaching more and more and feeling lonely if you're in the house all day.

Alex, midwife and mother to two children

EXERCISE 40: BUILD YOUR OWN COMMUNITY

This visualisation exercise can help you to identify who are the people that you feel supported by. Feeling held by a group of people that you trust and who you know you can call or connect with can make you feel supported and secure. Even if you never need to call them, just knowing they are there can feel good. Sit for a moment and identify people who:

- You feel comforted by.
- You feel loved by.
- Are free of judgement.
- You trust.
- Make you laugh.
- Would happily do your shopping.
- You would leave your baby with.

Make sure you also consider someone within the healthcare profession. If you feel you don't have these people in your life, ask yourself if you feel you need them. You may be perfectly content without that type of support in your life. If you feel you do, getting out to meet other mothers and people in your community can be so beneficial. Use the Bubble of Confidence and Calm (see page 138) for confidence, or the mini goal-setting (see page 118) to imagine yourself doing it, if you feel apprehensive. Some people I know also started volunteering in the community to meet other people and get involved in local events. You can find out more information about volunteering at your library, in your local newspaper or via your local council. I moved to a very rural area when my children were young and I knew no-one; my mother was 250 miles away. Meeting people through local groups was sometimes just what I needed, and I was always amazed by the kindness of people. I learned who the good babysitters were so I could have an hour off here and there, and a walk to the local butcher and greengrocer became a reassuringly familiar and chatty event. When I was too tired to do this, online supermarkets were brilliant at doing my shopping for me! I joined a tennis club where I met people who are still my friends 15 years on. People are there when you allow yourself to be open to connection. You never know who you might meet or start a conversation with!

You can download this as a blank worksheet and personalise it. Add extra information like contact numbers and pop it on your fridge so that you are reminded of the people you can call on.

Build your team

Who will listen?

Who can I trust with baby?

Who can fold my laundry & cook me a meal?

Who makes me feel loved?

Who makes me laugh?

Whose shoulder can I cry on?

From loneliness to aloneness

You can have the biggest circle of support imaginable but still feel loneliness. This may be because you are alone in your own, unique experience. With intense transitions and emotional change, it can be a very human thing to feel isolated; people may care and want to do everything they can to help, but they cannot be *in* the experience for you.

This is another one of those life lessons, and many, if not all, new parents will experience it in some way. With the right tools loneliness or aloneness can be a valuable experience; learning to sit with the experience of solitude will be something you can use throughout your life. Sometimes, when you are at home caring for your baby, it will be just the two of you, and this can be an adjustment, especially if you are used to a busy work environment.

Understanding the difference between loneliness and aloneness is important. Loneliness is intolerance to being alone, feeling emptiness, bored, longing for company and needing to fill a void. Those feelings may be uncomfortable, and rather than leaning into them, it can be easier to find things that distract you from it and push those feelings down. What if you choose instead to meet them? To turn towards them, being curious about them. This is acceptance; not turning away, but turning towards.

Tip: *You can get used to feeling alone by slowing down and using the Sensory Spotlight technique (see page 123). It can help you to connect to your space, and practised on a regular basis can help you to feel more comfortable in it.*

Instead of loneliness you can learn to cultivate a fulfilling experience of 'aloneness' – this is the ability to be comfortable with being alone with baby, and with your own feelings. Looking deeply in those moments can open up your world. Like petals on a flower opening up, these moments offer you an opportunity to witness the unfurling of a world within you and to dive into those depths fearlessly.

Nothing can give you peace but yourself.

Ralph Waldo Emerson

EXERCISE 41: PLUGGING INTO THE MOTHERSPHERE

This exercise can help you build a heart connection with other women all over the world who are experiencing the same things. Think of it as a 'mothersphere', a space where you can sit comfortably together in aloneness. It can be a joyful, loving, and energising experience. You can adopt this technique throughout your life for different situations.

1. Sit down with your feet on the ground, with your baby in your arms, or if they are sleeping, on your own.
2. Close your eyes and take a deep breath, and then breathing in 3 ... 2 ... 1 ..., and breathing out, relax ... relax ... relax ... Settle into the rhythm of your breath.
3. Imagine a golden light above your head.
4. With your next deep breath in, imagine that light moving down through your body.
5. Now breathe it out like a golden thread of light; keep breathing in and out until it is swirling in the room.
6. Now imagine the golden light drifting down the streets, with each breath moving up into the air, as if it is dancing down the streets, carried on the winds across the skies

and the seas, the continents, spreading and sparkling in the sun and moonlight.

7. Imagine that golden light reaching and swirling around other women with babies, feeling loneliness right now, all around the world. Notice that connection with those other women. Sit with those women just as you are in the moment you are in.

In the dark before the dawn
I am with you
The only sounds are the waking birds
The revellers returning to their beds
The workers waking from theirs
And us, the mothers
Wrapped around their babies
Halfway into sleep
Connected by an invisible thread
And the moon.

Summary

Cultivating connections with family, friends and community can help support you in the year ahead. You want people who you trust, feel safe with, and most of all, who feel easy to be with. Remember you can build new friendships and new communities. Use the hypnosis mini-goal setting (see page 118) to rehearse going to new places in your mind and to help you build confidence. Explore the differences between loneliness and aloneness, being kind to yourself in the stillness. And why not try to tap into the mothersphere.

15

Tough Days

Perhaps it takes courage to raise children?

John Steinbeck

There are going to be days that challenge you, days that are tougher than others. It may be early on, or it may be as you are emerging from the newborn stage at around four, six or nine months. That's parenthood; it is unpredictable and yet also relentless. There will be days when you feel pulled in a hundred different directions. It may be things within your little family unit like illness, teething or exhaustion, or it could be things outside of your family that throw you off course, such as finances, jobs, friends or childcare issues. Sometimes you might just have a day when you feel you want to throw a blanket over your head and hibernate.

'Breathe in, breathe out … in this moment I am alive.'

I did a forgiveness meditation/relaxation after really tough days. Forgiveness is a really important practice for any new mother.

Keira, mother to two children

> **Tip:** *If you want to skip the reading pages here, and need help right now, go straight to the* **Calm Breath** *download to catch a breath and boost your wellbeing.*

Take it moment by moment

Drop everything that is unnecessary. Everything. If it means letting people down, apologise and rearrange. If you find this hard to do, ask yourself the following questions:

- Do you need to do this task right now?
- Can you take a rain check and postpone your plans?
- Does it really matter?

This last one is my absolute favourite when I think I've messed up or am pushing myself to go to something, or am letting something go. I use this often. If you ask this question and start off on a train of thought about whether it really matters, stop! Come back to your breath, saying the words in your mind as you breathe in and out:

'Breathing in and breathing out.'

When your mind is focused on your breath and these words in your mind, it cannot start galloping in the past or future. It gives you the option to stay in the present, uncluttered by thoughts. If there are any days you need to find space to breathe, today is one of those days. The breath creates the space it needs. Right now, just allow yourself to be with your breath in the present. **PRESS PAUSE.**

> **Tip:** *Use your* **Calm Breath**: *'Breathing in, 3 ... 2 ... 1 ..., breathing out, relax ... relax ... relax ... ' in moments when you remember. Just stopping for 10-second pauses with the intention to breathe and connect will help you.*

EXERCISE 42: GLASS BALLS AND RUBBER BALLS

As a new mother, you are always juggling. What if you changed the way you saw those balls? Imagine them as rubber balls and glass balls. The glass balls are the balls that you absolutely cannot drop and the rubber balls are ones that you think you have to keep juggling, but actually, if you dropped them they would bounce back. Depending on what is happening in your life, the glass balls and rubber balls will be different and might change.

When you are feeling very tired and you just want to get off the wheel, use this exercise to work out which jobs, people and tasks are your glass balls and which are your rubber balls. Be as tough as you can. If you need more balls, add them!

- Make a list in your mind or on paper or in a journal of five things that are glass balls. These could be feeding baby and you, taking a shower, hugging your partner, doing the nursery run.
- Make a list of things that are rubber balls. These could be checking social media, making a complicated new recipe, or ironing.

How to
Juggle

Some days you will have to push on through and somehow just make it to the end.

I'm not going to lie, the beginning was tough. My toddler was too young to understand that I couldn't tend to his every need. The hardest was when they both needed my full attention at the same time. It's funny how you quickly learn tips and tricks along the way.

The wrap sling was amazing for hands-free toddler entertaining, as was the stash of board books during those longer early feeds. My toddler knew that was his time for mother's stories. A few weeks in and colic struck full force! This was all new to me as none of my others had it. To get through this phase was pure survival. I said to myself if we get through the day and we're all alive then that's a job well done! Lowering my standards was one of the best things I did. It was hard at first but the liberation of letting go and saying it really doesn't matter gave immediate relief!

Laura, mother to three children

If your baby is ill

If your baby is unwell, whether it's a common cold or something more serious, your routine will be disrupted. Accepting this disruption may be all you can do – give yourself permission to focus on what's essential. Here are a couple of things that might help:

- Ask someone from your support circle for help.
- Use the Bubble of Confidence and Calm (see page 138).
- Prepare to be a human cushion until your baby is better!

When your baby is with you, and comforted by you, they feel safer and more secure. This in turn reduces the level of stress, which can then aid healing. Babies, like all humans, recover faster when they feel loved and nurtured. Your baby will feel like an extension of you more than ever when they are ill.

'I let go of everything else and allow myself to be what baby needs right now.'

If you are ill

If you can get help, great. But sometimes you have to keep going, and yes it can be hard. But these days will pass – on these days remind yourself that you *can* do this. If you are at home with baby, have a duvet day, and drop as much as you can to allow this to happen. If baby is crying and you are ill, use the track from the chapter on crying (see page 152) to give you an extra boost.

> **Tip:** *There will be days when you need a break; just do what you can to keep afloat. Let go of guilt. If it's basic food for breakfast, lunch and dinner, and then lots of TV, then so be it.*

Baths with candlelight had such a soothing effect for me. I did this particularly if I was crying. I would give myself time to feel sad/guilty/angry/overwhelmed etc., and cry it out into the bath for as long as I needed. Then I would visualise all those feelings draining away with the bath water. This worked so well. I would even thank the bath and water for its holding/cleansing/time.

Brigid, mother to two children

Mini-tools for a quick fix

When time is short, life is full, energy depleted and motivation is low, having a bag of mini-tools that you can dip in on days like this can make all the difference. Some of these don't take any extra effort, they just shift your lens so you can refresh your view, or nurture you in a very basic way. You may want to add some of these to your self-care rainbow (see page 54).

'Sometimes I feel vulnerable and that's ok, I give myself permission to slow down today.'

CHANGING PERSPECTIVE

If you are finding the day emotionally tough, or you are feeling unmotivated or apathetic, you can get a boost by getting a change of scene, or perspective. If you are out walking to work or to the shops, take a different route, and use the mindful walking on page 143 to connect with that route.

If you are breastfeeding, change the chair you feed in so you have a different view, perhaps looking out of a different window or in a different room.

USE YOUR INNER CONTROL ROOM

Close your eyes and imagine you have your own inner control room in your mind. If you had one what would it look like? Bring that control room to life. Now think about what needs adjusting at the moment. Do you need more patience, more motivation? Do you need to switch off something or switch something on? Or do you just need to empty the trash can in your mind? Your control room can adjust all your feelings, whether physical or emotional. Adjust the controls, turning up what you need, and turning down or getting rid of what you don't.

TA-DA LISTS

Take a moment to think about all the things you *have* achieved today. It's likely that you forget how much you actually do! If you aren't the type of person who writes lists but juggles in their head, take a moment at the end of a tough day to do this. I do these all the time!

- Think of all the little things you have done that day, such as feeding, soothing, school runs, laundry, made lunch etc.
- Write them all down.
- Now put a line through them all.
- You completed your ta-da list today!

FRESH AIR

Go outside. If you have a garden or balcony, go out to it and breathe deeply. Stretch your arms up high to the sky. Come back to your breathing, breathing in and breathing out. Notice your feet on the ground. Feel expansive and strong as your body connects with the earth and the sky. If you don't have an outdoor space, take baby with you in the pushchair or sling and set out for a few minutes in your local park; I am sure you can find a quiet spot for a moment to stretch.

MAKE A CUP OF TEA

It may be a very British thing, but I believe a cup of tea fixes everything. Douglas Adams, author of *The Hitchhiker's Guide to the Galaxy*, famously loved the restorative nature of a cup of tea. In his book he had an invention called 'The Infinite Improbability Drive', which was fuelled by a really hot cup of tea.

Take a moment to drink your tea mindfully. Drink with awareness, noticing the warmth of the tea, the weight of the mug in your hand, the flavours of the tea, and imagine the ground in which the tea grew, the sun that warmed it and the person who picked it. Most of all, have gratitude that you are drinking a hot cup of tea!

If your baby is using a cup, why not give them a cup with their drink in and do this together.

DANCE AND SING

Get your body moving. Put some music on and dance. Even if it's 6am, some of your favourite music can uplift you and ground you in your body. As you dance, notice the freedom of your movement and connect with your body. Don't let your mind be carried off to other things; pay attention to your movement. You can do this on your own or with baby. Or sing loudly and expressively; or dance and sing at the same time!

I used to play a game with my children called, 'We're living in a musical'; if I was tired and run-down I would just sing what I was doing, then as they got older I would add a chorus for them to join in. For example, the chorus would be: 'It's breakfast time, it's breakfast time, grab your spoons it's breakfast time!' I am not a creative genius or a pitch-perfect singer at 6.30am, but a rousing rendition of: 'I'm boiling the milk for your porridge' always broke the monotony. It really worked at getting me out of my slump and my babies thought it was hilarious – when your baby starts laughing, it's contagious. If this isn't for you, here is a list of music suggested by mothers for the first year – bit.ly/mindfulmamma.

SMILE

Even if you don't feel like it, smile. Do it now. When you smile, the physical act of smiling releases the chemicals serotonin and dopamine in your brain. Now breathe deeply, smile widely, and keep smiling, giving your brain an opportunity to release these chemicals. Soon you will be feeling happier for real. Another way to release these happy hormones is to be playful with your baby. Hold your baby with you in front of a mirror and smile, keep smiling, point at your smile and point at their smile. See what happens!

> Sometimes your joy is the source of your smile,
> but sometimes your smile can be the source of
> your joy.
>
> Thich Nhat Hanh

JOY IS FREE

Financial pressures can be a worry when you have had a baby. Things can be tight for a while so it's important to think about how much is free. Think about the things that bring you joy, the little things, like being out in the sunshine, snuggling up on the sofa with your baby, a hug or a bath. Research activities that are free in your area, such as baby groups, events and exhibitions.

Write a list of the top 10 things that are free, and which can enrich your day. Refer to this list when you need a boost, or you can add it to your self-care rainbow (see page 54).

1.   6.

2.   7.

3.   8.

4.   9.

5.   10.

I notice thoughts like clouds
Form
Take shape
And let them drift through
Knowing that just above the clouds
The sky is always blue

Zöe Strickland, mother of three children

CONNECT WITH A FRIEND

Connecting with a friend who lifts you up and who you can be completely honest with can help. You can cry, laugh, watch a film together or even help out by watching each other's baby while the other person has a nap! Who is that person for you?

Summary

On tough days, bring it back to basics. Focus on caring for you and your baby in the simplest way possible. Give yourself permission to miss a group or cancel an appointment. It's okay – there will be other times to do those things. Do what is most important on that day and use some of the mini-tools above to connect with your mind and body. You *will* get through this day, like you got through others in the past. Just take it moment by moment. Speak to someone if you are having lots of these days and feel you need some more support (see page 120).

part four

Embracing the Mother
in You

16

Who am I?

The woman you are now, is the woman you have always been. And more.

In our culture there is a strong focus on the physical aspects of birth, and very little that teaches us about the psychological changes. The adjustment to motherhood is complex and multi-layered; you might be aware or feel the changes, but it can be hard to make sense of them. Sometimes you may feel as if you are clinging on to threads of who you think you are. Even though you may have been preparing for motherhood for a long time, it can still catch you off guard.

Although you may have experienced other major shifts in your life, *nothing* is like becoming a mother. You even have a new name: Mother! Your partner too, will also have a new name.

> When the midwife came over with my baby and said: 'Here's Mother', my instinct was to turn around and look for my mother at the door, until it caught up with me and I realised that I was now Mother.
>
> *Jenny, mother to three children*

A new you

Although it may not feel it right now, this is an opportunity for personal development, both emotionally and spiritually.

Any time of transition and transformation is, by nature, challenging, because it takes you beyond your comfort zone and asks you to redefine who you think you are. This can be deeply uncomfortable, but it's an inevitable part of change.

> *'I lean into the experience of change, allowing comfort where there is discomfort.'*

As a culture, we may be more familiar with midlife or adolescence as times of growth and change, but becoming a mother and emerging into motherhood is an often forgotten and unrecognised point of growth. We understand that adolescence brings external and internal physical changes, some of which are happening in the brain. This is also true of motherhood; these physical changes add to the intensity of your experience, and you may be able to sense them, but not be able to identify them. Expressions like: 'I don't recognise myself,' or 'I feel I've lost a part of myself,' or 'I don't know who I am any more' reveal this shift in the brain. Imagine your brain as a map to which new paths, roads and motorways have been added. The map is not the same as before but you will learn how to navigate this map with ease, just as you have at other times in your life; you just need time to familiarise yourself with it.

In adolescence you may have experienced greasy hair, spots, body changes and hormonal swings and these are all normal, even if we didn't feel comfortable with them. You may have made allowances around these changes, and others may have too. With motherhood we tend to be far less forgiving of the changes happening. What if this were a recognised stage in our development? What if it had a name, like adolescence, or menopause? Would that make a difference?

Well, there *is* a name for becoming a mother and all the changes that come with that: 'matrescense'. I hope that our society will become more aware, more accepting and more supportive of this stage.

In many ways matrescense is an even more powerful experience than adolescence, as the shift takes place over such a short space of time. The nine months of pregnancy can be very focused on the physical aspects, especially the birth itself, with little time given to reflect on the deeper psychological shifts. In all the focus around birth, the meaning of becoming a mother can be lost. But the birth of a mother is a miraculous, powerful and wonderful thing. It is part of life and you are part of a lineage of other strong women, of mothers stretching far back, including women from whom you inherited strength and wisdom. **PRESS PAUSE.**

'In this moment I lovingly connect with the
woman I was, the woman I am now and the
woman I will be.'

The mother emerging in you

As the new mother emerges in you, you may not have time to consciously reflect on the thoughts and feelings that arise with the shift into motherhood. This may be expressed in tears and very powerful feelings in the early weeks. Your focus may be on ensuring that your basic needs are met, such as food, rest and hygiene – the fourth trimester can leave little space for much else. Knowing this and leaning into it with acceptance is your most powerful rescue remedy. It helps you to ride out the exhaustion of the early weeks. You may not be able to do some of the things you loved and that made you feel like you for a while, but if you have completed your self-care rainbow there will be small things you can do to keep yourself connected with who you feel you are.

> I joined a gym with a crèche; as part of my £50-a-month membership I got two hours a day of crèche time. I went once or twice a week and used the time to do a yoga class, go for a run on the machines, have a child-free meal in the cafe or just fall asleep in the health suite!
>
> *Rachel, mother to one child*

As the weeks go on it can feel as if the fourth trimester fog is lifting – however, it's not a magical fog that disappears at the 12-week mark; it can linger for a while, hanging around sometimes for six months or longer. Let's take a moment to think about times in the past when you have experienced a transition. Connect with your **Calm Breath** for a moment and reflect on those times:

1. What did you let go of?
2. How did you grow?
3. If you were to look back and say one thing that would make things easier, what would it be?
4. Close your eyes. Imagine your emotions like a river and that you are a reed in the riverbed, surrendering to the water as the river rushes through. Sometimes the currents are stronger, sometimes the river flows more gently. Can you be like the reed, observing the flow of the water around you, not being carried away with it?

We do not grow absolutely, chronologically.
We grow sometimes in one dimension, and not
in another; unevenly. We grow partially. We are
relative. We are mature in one realm, childish in
another. The past, present and future mingle and
pull us backward, forward or fix us in the present.
We are made up of layers, cells, constellations.

Anaïs Nin

I don't feel like 'me' any more

One of the first things you will learn in the early days of the fourth trimester is that everything you thought made you *you*, such as your job, going to the gym, having a drink with your colleagues after work, eating out, reading the Sunday papers, painting, crafting, travelling, going out with friends, has been usurped by baby's needs. If you are unable to take part in the things that define you, you may wonder if you really are you. People often say to me: 'I'm not me any more.'

You *are* you, and more.

When freedom is considered to be one of the conditions for happiness, it can feel like a bereavement for the life you had before when it seems curtailed. You may feel trapped or not able to put your finger on why you feel loss. If this sounds familiar, stop! Take a deep breath, **PRESS PAUSE.**

Now allow yourself to liberate your thinking and to re-define this stage in your life as a big rollercoaster of love. The love of change, the love of who you are becoming, the love of your baby, the love of all the emotions that are bubbling under the surface and the feelings that arise from them. Love is powerful and it can take you anywhere; it doesn't have to be twee and sentimental, it can embrace all of feeling, all of experience. You can choose to approach everything, including the changes in yourself, with love.

You can build on who you are, learn more about yourself, and grow into a bigger version of yourself. Many women become stronger versions of themselves after having children.

> We are volcanoes. When we women offer our
> experience as our truth, as human truth… There
> are new mountains.
>
> Ursula Le Guin

Tap into the heart of who you are and decide how you choose to approach this new chapter in your life. Remember, you are not defined by the experiences that you have had, but by how you approached those experiences. Life is always changing; from the moment you were born you have had experiences, some of them familiar and comfortable, others not so. The ways you have spent your time become habits because you discovered you enjoyed them and they made you feel good.

If how you used to spend your time doesn't define who you are, then what does? The values you live by. Your values are portable throughout your life whatever happens; they are the authentic you. Research tells us that connection with values is the best predictor of future behaviour and action. By connecting with your values you are more likely to pick up on habits and hobbies that feel consistent with who you are. Values are adaptable to any experience, especially to parenting.

> 'Each and every day I feel more connected
> to my values, and as I connect to my values I
> return to myself, stronger than I was before.'

When you know your values, you can apply them to the cascade of new experiences that arise every moment, of every day; they are part of your authentic self. When you parent with authenticity at your heart, it feels honest and best of all, it feels like you.

EXERCISE 43: KNOWING YOUR MOTHERING VALUES

This hypnosis visualisation will help you connect to your mothering instincts and values.

- Start by focusing on your **Calm Breath**, taking nice deep breaths. This exercise needs you to get into a space that feels a little like daydreaming.
- Think of an occasion, perhaps an experience at work or at home, where you have felt really fulfilled afterwards. It may have been a: 'Wow I did that!' moment.
- Play that experience over and over like a film in your mind, really focusing on the feeling.
- Now think about the values that you brought into that experience. How did you approach it? It can be things like courage, tenacity, warmth, determination, efficiency, compassion, thoughtfulness, patience, but really think of your own values, as those will be most authentic to you.

Write those values down here:

1.
2.
3.

Add more if you wish.

If you like, write these values on a piece of paper and have them somewhere you can see them on a regular basis. When you are faced with a challenge you can say: 'I am going to face this moment with …', adding one of your values.

The things that matter to you, still matter

Doing things that are familiar to you is important, not because they make you who you are, but because they can have a soothing effect. Hobbies and interests can meet your need for self-care because they make you feel happy in body and mind. This is why these things can become part of your self-care routine.

Once the fog starts to lift, you may find it easier to reintroduce the things that are important to you. Understand that there may be less time for a little while, but don't entirely stop doing the things you love. If you used to go to the gym three times a week, or a music group once a week, how can you make time for it now? Even if it's once a month, it's worth it. Ask people from your support circle if they can watch baby while you do something for yourself, however small. I used to ask my friend to keep an eye on my son while I nipped out to get some shopping and have a walk. A simple thing like getting a pint of milk felt like a day out and the exercise got my endorphins flowing.

This is a point to refer back to your self-care rainbow on page 54. Think of things that you enjoy that take just 5 minutes, up to 30 minutes or even longer. The trick is to make it something simple and achievable.

I was fortunate enough to have a postnatal craft group local to me run by midwives. I initially attended while pregnant and really enjoyed the different activities we did. Pom-pom balls were made, as were friendships. Having your conscious mind focused on an activity with a cup of tea and slice of cake gives room for conversation. I've found it so much easier to bond with others when we're sat round a table together and engaging our creativity. I guess it's kind of like a meditation in some ways and you're all doing it together. It's become my weekly safe place and the ladies who attend have all become friends. Really meaningful friendships as well. So not only do your friendships gow, but the friendships of the babies too.

Keira, mother to two children

Find your tribe

When you start to get out and about, you may find that your priorities have changed. Your friendship group may shift and change. There are so many things you can get involved in during maternity leave that can help you to create opportunities for you to feel more like yourself.

'As I connect with the world around me, I become aware of opportunities to meet my creative, emotional and physical needs.'

More cafés, restaurants and clubs than ever are making it easier for mothers to meet and take part in activities and events. From mindful walks to daytime nightclubs, be creative and find something you enjoy. What did you enjoy before, what made you feel good? I love a hugely popular initiative that was started by Lorna Hayward called 'Pizzups'. Recognising that women wanted an opportunity to go out and let their hair down and have time for themselves, she set this up. The idea is great as it provides an opportunity for a good night out and says to each and every mother who goes: 'Hey you are still you!' and, 'You are not alone.' Here is Lorna's story of why she started Pizzups:

I started Pizzups to fulfil my own needs after feelings of isolation and trying to adapt to motherhood as best I can, and, well, I still need to be a part of something. It's about putting aside everything for just one night (and possibly the morning after) for me, for us and for the camaraderie that comes with partying alongside women on the same path as you. It's pretty magical. I always liken it to a good wedding – decent food, lots of booze and excellent tunes. It helps that my husband is also a DJ. I'm still utterly blown away at the number of wonderwomen who want to buy tickets and turn up on the night.

Lorna Hayward, mother to three children

Just because you have had a baby doesn't mean that you need to stop doing the things you love; see if you can do them with your baby. I stopped playing tennis when I was pregnant, and didn't start playing again until my boys were older. It is one of my biggest regrets. My mother was very different; she had me sitting up at the side of the court while she played, then as I started to walk, she would have me on court picking balls up, and before long I was in the tots group while she sat and had a cup of tea.

Tip: *Find activities that fulfil a need in you. Baby massage and baby yoga are all great, but is there something that you love to do that you can do with baby? Baby will learn about the world around them through watching you do it. They don't need socialising yet, and are pretty portable, so take advantage of that while you can!*

When I had Ellie I missed my book group at work, so I found a book group at a local library during the day and began to attend. I was the youngest there by a long way! I didn't always get time to read the book either, but it was great. The women there had had children, and had seen their grandchildren grow. They were encouraging and supportive, and they loved holding Ellie too. I was doing something I loved, I was using my brain, and it was great to connect with others who were outside of the usual baby toddler groups.

Alice, mother to one child

Summary

Not being able to follow the pattern of your life as you knew it can be unsettling. So one solution is to change your perspective! This is a period of growth; you will learn new things about yourself, develop new skills and tap into resources you never knew you had. Use this time to identify and define your values, as these are the constant throughout your life, and it will feel reassuring to connect with those as you emerge into motherhood. Make time for your self-care, even if it is only 10 minutes a day. And when ready, reconnect with the things that you enjoy doing.

17

Body Positive

Life should not be a journey to the grave with the
intention of arriving safely in a pretty and well-
preserved body, but rather to skid in broadside
in a cloud of smoke, thoroughly used-up, totally
worn-out, and loudly proclaiming: "Wow! What a
Ride!"

Hunter S. Thompson

Your body has been through so many changes, it needs
kindness, gratitude and love in the first year. Body
issues are high on the cultural agenda at the moment, and
what we see in the media often drives unrealistic expectations for new mothers. Your body, right now, is the body of
a mother. A warm, nourishing, nurturing, soft, loving mother.
It's exactly what your baby needs.

'When I see my body I notice and embrace all
the things that make me a mother.'

There is the old adage: 'Nine months on and nine months off.'
In my case, and I think for most women, it was longer. Why not
give yourself permission to take the pressure off? This time is
short in the scheme of parenting, so instead of focusing on
what your body is not doing, think about what it is doing.

Take a moment and name at least one extraordinary thing that your body has done or is doing right now in this moment. Why not try to remember to do this at any time during the day. If you find your internal narrator talking you down, change the narrative by naming an amazing thing your body is doing in that moment.

> I can't believe my body grew a baby and fed it for nine months. I look at my tummy (with stretchmarks) and boobs (which are less full) and think: 'Wow, you're amazing!' I never tried to make that happen, my body just did it.
>
> *Hannah, mother to one child*

BELLY

B Breathe deeply

E Embrace the changes

L Look deeply

L Love fully

Y Yield to the experience

Give yourself time to adjust

Your body is not just what you see on the outside; it's a repository of experience. It holds memories of love, trauma, stress, strength, power and pleasure. What you see on the outside gives a little away; the marks on your skin tell the story of your life, each lump, bump, scar and line is like a word on a page.

> **Tip:** *Soften your language. Instead of calling them stretchmarks, why not call them your mamma map or love lines?*

'I relax and soften into my body, thanking it for all it does for me.'

Your body may feel unfamiliar to you at the moment – it's a big change going from being not pregnant, to pregnant and not pregnant again, in the space of nine months. Your breasts may be heavy with milk, and your belly will be soft and squidgy. You have grown and birthed a baby. Just as your body got on with adjusting and changing to accommodate a human being, it will now be adjusting back, rebalancing and reorganising. For more on healing, read Chapter 7, and allow yourself time to heal in the best way that your body can.

I always see the mamma belly as an amazing design of nature! Just think about where it is, and how content your baby feels snuggled against you in their perfectly designed nest, easing the transition from womb to world.

Nature's
Perfect nest

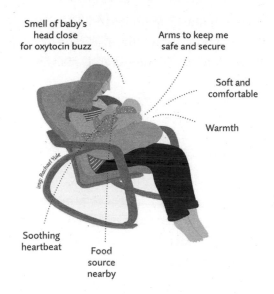

Smell of baby's head close for oxytocin buzz

Arms to keep me safe and secure

Soft and comfortable

Warmth

img: Rachael Yule

Soothing heartbeat

Food source nearby

> Pregnancy, birth and breastfeeding completely changed my relationship with my body, for the better. Suddenly, what it looked like was so much less important than the amazing things it could do.
>
> *Guinevere, mother to three children*

Exercise and motivation

Postnatally, exercise should not be focused on getting slimmer, but on your health and wellbeing. Many women I know who exercise a lot are keen to get back to it after pregnancy, as they recognise the benefits to their wellbeing and enjoy the endorphins it releases. In the previous chapter we explored the concept of self; if this is one of the hobbies and habits you enjoy and identify with, then great. Usually you can return to exercise after the six-week check. But you can be your own judge too; if you don't feel ready, don't rush it. Start off small and build up. There are plenty of ways to introduce fitness back into your life (see resources, page 267). Be creative about how you can adapt your old exercise routine; you could try a version at home while baby is playing, or even with baby.

If you want to exercise because you know it makes you feel better, but are struggling with motivation or time, use this hypnosis visualisation:

Imagine yourself preparing, going through the exercise, and focus on how good you feel afterwards. If you are someone for whom exercise is usually a big part of their life, you will be able to step into this feeling very easily. If not, it might need more practice!

Waking up positive with a coffee and a workout starts the day well. It improves my metabolism and that in itself is a great endorphin start to the day! Doing it makes me feel good for having done something that day. When Tillie was tiny, it started with just pelvic floor and light cardio and I gradually introduced weights when the doctor gave me the all-clear. 45 minutes, three times a week is actually really achievable around baby as they nap or play. Then if they get fed up, I use them as my weights, doing squats and lunges while holding them. They love that interaction. It's all about mind-set and waking up with a positive attitude. Walking is also a great exercise and a morning walk is just another way of boosting those endorphins. I also make sure that I drink a lot of water and eat well for energy.

Emily, mother to three children

EXERCISE 44: MIRROR OF SELF-LOVE

Loving your body is one of the most basic forms of self-care and compassion. Your body is you. What do you say to yourself when you look in the mirror? What do you see? Do you just see the physical body, or do you see the whole of you?

With this exercise I want you to stand in front of a mirror and say out loud everything that is positive about who you are, and about your body. Look not just at 'what' you see, but also 'who' you see.

Think about how the people you love (and who love you) see you. Your children, your friends and your partner. Who do they see and what do they love about you? Ask them if you have to!

Look in the mirror and think of your:

- Characteristics
- Strengths
- Parts of your body that you love
- Parts of your body that you have gratitude for.

If you find your thoughts drifting to what you don't like, come back to the phrase: 'Be your own best friend'. This can be a challenging exercise but is really worth doing, as not only does it help you focus on the positive, but it can highlight how much you need to work on it too.

Tip: *If you have a large mirror, write on all these positive characteristics with a water-soluble marker pen. Or, if you want to write positive messages on your mirror with permanent marker, go right ahead!*

Summary

Your body will have changed, so allow it time to adjust. Be gentle and kind to yourself. Rest, and allow your baby and your mind space in those early days; your body will follow. Think about the incredible things your body has done and thank it for what it has achieved. Even if you are itching to get back to exercise after your six-week check, don't rush. And if you need a little motivation, use the mini-goal hypnosis exercise to go for a walk, or to do whatever you know makes you feel good.

18

Forgiveness and Letting Go

Forgiveness is not an occasional act, it is a
constant attitude.

Martin Luther King Jr.

earning forgiveness and letting go can be the simplest,
but also the hardest thing to learn as a parent. Every
parent wants to do their best, but the market is flooded
with books telling us how parents f*** us up! We are also
bombarded with images everywhere of women perfectly
balancing everything. What's a parent to do? Everyone
you know will be having a different experience; you will all
parent differently, cope differently, enjoy different aspects
of parenting and find some stages easier than others. Some
mothers will be naturals at the baby stage and may struggle
at toddler stage. I loved all stages, but some I found easier
than others.

The point is, there is no perfect way to parent, and some
days you will get it wrong, very wrong. But that's okay. Often
doing something wrong the first time helps you to do it
better the second time.

'I am learning to forgive myself,
and to let go of guilt.'

In moments when you wish you could take back what you just did, you can choose to apologise, forgive yourself, and let it go. You can't change what has happened, but you can make it an ending and create a new beginning. All experiences are a learning experience. You can't see into the future, and often you are winging it.

> True forgiveness is saying thank you for that experience.
>
> Oprah Winfrey

I would do (and still do) a daily practice of compassion. Compassion for myself, for others and sometimes for a specific thing going on. I do this either by breathing compassion in or out. This is simple, yet after doing it regularly it can invoke compassion even when feeling lost, low, stressed, worried or anxious. It becomes forgiving and uplifting. I have to say, some days this is a ten-times-a-day practice!

Lola, mother to two children

EXERCISE 45: FORGIVING YOURSELF

Ho'oponopono is a traditional Hawaiian practice of forgiveness and reconciliation. It embraces forgiveness, gratitude and love. You can direct it to a person or to a feeling. Put your hand on your heart while you say it:

I'm sorry
Please forgive me
Thank you
I love you

Can you say this to yourself when standing in front of a mirror? It's not always easy to bear witness to the actions and behaviour from which guilt arises, but it can be very powerful.

Are you a 'perfect' or a 'good-enough' mother?

The correct answer to this is, of course, 'A good-enough mother'! You may feel that you need to strive to be the perfect mother, but there *is* no perfect; there is only good enough – and that's enough for your baby. Even if you have days when you think your good enough is not good enough, let me tell you that it is. If anyone thinks I am the perfectly calm, mindful mamma 100 per cent of the time, they don't know me!

Dr D. W. Winnicott has saved so many mothers from the extremes of guilt with the 'good enough' research. This model recognised that even though a mother would strive to provide physical care, emotional warmth and love, she would also naturally fail sometimes, unwittingly unable to meet the needs of her baby. These moments create opportunities for baby to begin to develop a sense of 'me' and 'not me' and learn to adapt and cope in the world. 'Failing' to meet a need is just those ordinary, everyday things such as when you are driving to pick up other children from school, baby is crying so you just can't meet that need in that moment. It's reality!

When you accept that you can just be with your baby, not striving to be more than you need to be in this moment, then you can lovingly greet the authentic mother inside you.

Sometimes life will feel perfect, and sometimes it won't. You don't need to read a book to know that, do you? Your baby is learning the same lesson. 'Good enough' gives your baby the opportunities to develop resilience and to become independent as they discover their own way in the world. They will learn how to navigate life from what you are teaching them, not just your behaviour, but also how you regulate yourself and respond to others.

Sometimes being a mother is doing nothing for a day, just sitting there, holding your baby. So many parents I know feel pressured to get out and do lots of clubs and events with baby, and feel guilty if they don't. If you don't feel like doing that, let it go. You are doing, and giving, your baby so much by just being with them. This is valuable time to rest and connect.

Take a moment to hold your baby, or if they are asleep, imagine holding them. Think about what they are feeling; they feel safe, loved, secure and happy. If you are feeling overwhelmed by trying to do too much, say to yourself: 'This is enough for today.'

'As I sit here and cuddle my beautiful baby, I connect and meet the needs of both my baby and the beautiful mother in me.'

Tip: *Check in with your feelings by using the CALMER Way exercise on page 151 if you are getting overwhelming feelings of guilt.*

When you feel like you are doing nothing
You are doing everything

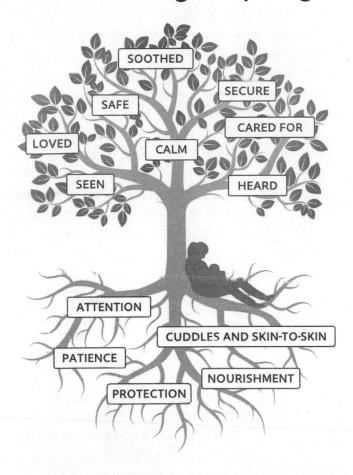

The idea of 'identity', after our core being has been rocked by the enormity of birth, is one I still struggle to put into words. When you have a baby, whether it's your first or fifth, each time your soul swells to make room to love another. Each pregnancy is completely unique to those experiencing it. How we come back to ourselves after that rocking is individual. Strip it back to your basic emotional needs of community, connection and to be witnessed just as you are. What we go through as women, and as intricate families when we expand, deserves a readjustment phase. The fourth trimester is a raw and peeled-back existence; the mother in you has been born too, and she may take some getting used to. Give yourself permission to allow what comes up to the surface a chance to be allowed. I really worked around the word 'forgiveness' and affirmed it to myself with a Forgiveness track by Sophie. Whatever had happened that day, the good parts and the bad parts, they were consciously acknowledged by just taking those five minutes. There's power in that. My 'golden nugget' for this time is to know that your baby loves you for you, for being the constant presence in their lives, and for making the world a little less scary. You may feel like the work you are doing isn't being seen, but those little eyes are watching. You are enough, all the parts of you, and I see you. Mothers of all kinds, everywhere, before and after us, see you and the incredibly important work you are doing. If you have days where you don't see yourself, please know we see you. I found great comfort in affirming this to myself.

Keira, mother to two children

Ambivalence and guilt

Ambivalence is when you have mixed or contradictory feelings about your needs and your baby's needs. It is a common aspect of parenting; you love your baby but dislike being woken frequently at night when you need sleep. You may be desperate for baby to fall asleep and then, when they do, all you want to do is stare at them, pick them up and cuddle them. You can feel frustration and love, resentment and content-ment, incapable and able, all at the same time. If you put into a search engine: 'I hate being a mother,' you will find millions of responses, but often those same women would do anything for their children, and they would feel terrible guilt if their children would ever sense or know that they felt this way.

Although common to all parents, ambivalence can give rise to feelings of unhappiness, anxiety and unkind thoughts towards your baby (such as: 'Will you just stop crying?'), and one reason is because it's not spoken about enough. I often speak to women who find it very difficult to voice these feelings because they feel that they are expected to love unconditionally, to be nurturing and kind all of the time. You may do your best to behave perfectly towards your children, and it may be what you present to the world, most of the time, but it may not be what you *feel* all the time.

This conflict can sometimes be a hiccup in how you want to parent. If it's a constant internal dialogue it can be exhaust-ing and confusing. However, suppressing those feelings can become an even bigger burden. One way that you can free yourself from this pattern of thinking is to practise accept-ance and forgiveness. Paying attention to those feelings, however uncomfortable, allows you to release the emotional charge in them. Having those feelings heard, whether by you or someone else, gives them space to exist. Name them, and then let them go in the moments that they arise.

Can you, as a mother, be of two minds? Can you recognise that those feelings are normal and use the simple practice of 'naming' to find a place between them? To know frustration and to accept it? To know love and to accept it? To know that all of this can be normal? **PRESS PAUSE.**

EXERCISE 46: NAME IT TO TAME IT

One way of finding a way through guilt is to name the feeling, acknowledge it and then let it go. It's all you need to do. No explanation needed. It may be a feeling of guilt, anger, frustration, sadness. It may be love, happiness or kindness. You can practise this exercise with all your feelings:

- As a feeling rises within you, acknowledge it and name it.
- Put your hand on your heart and say 'hello'. You may want to imagine giving that feeling a hug.
- And then send it on its way.

Try it with whatever emotion you are experiencing now.

> **Tip:** *Learn to see feelings as active participants in your parenting journey. They become 'people' you meet on your path, sometimes familiar, sometimes not. Just say hello to them and then walk on by.*

Letting go

Being able to let go of things quickly and easily is sometimes easier said than done. Yet, the more you do it the easier it becomes. You can't change the past, but you can begin to change the future right now. Learning to let go will be one of your most powerful parenting tools, and now is the time to start practising it. This can be a resoundingly liberating way to live.

'Emotional load' is like a heavy backpack that you carry around. When you turn away from a feeling instead of facing it, it sits within you, and as those feelings collect they build up an emotional charge – this charge can explode suddenly and without warning when it just gets too much. When it reaches capacity, something very small and uneventful could set off the explosion! It can be exhausting carrying all those feelings and emotion around. Many hypnosis visualisations around letting go focus on imagery such as taking off a heavy bag or weeding gardens and igniting bonfires of autumnal leaves. The type of language used during a therapy session may focus on lightness, space and freedom.

Regularly using breathing, visualisations and mindfulness means that you can learn to reduce your load before you become overwhelmed. This way you will find it much easier to cope and stay calm in moments that otherwise may have been challenging. This is why a small daily practice is a good habit to get into. When my children were babies, and I was exhausted and unable to manage anything else, I just put a guided visualisation on, like the **Forgiveness and Letting Go** download in the exercise below.

Affirmations are useful to have when you feel that emotional load or charge building up; they can help you physically let go of the things you are holding on to. This affirmation is one of the most popular affirmations from my first book and I wanted you to have it here too. I use it myself, all the time.

'As I breathe in I relax, as I breathe out I let go.'

At the root of letting go is forgiveness. It is such a powerful act. Forgiving yourself, and those around you, is an important value to learn to live by. Perhaps think about adding it to your list of values in the exercise on page 229? Over time this may be an idea that you can teach to your child/ren too, to help them develop resilience.

EXERCISE 47: FORGIVENESS AND LETTING GO

Download this track (see page 8) and play it whenever you need help with giving forgiveness. It's a simple hypnosis visualisation that will help you to let go of anything that is upsetting or worrying you, or it can just be a simple letting go at the end of each busy day. When you release things from the past, you have more capacity to deal with the things that will come in the future.

Summary

Be kind to yourself; you are emerging and learning as a mother. It is normal to get angry, frustrated and impatient. Your children, family and friends are privy to your vulnerabilities. Don't pretend they don't see them! There will be days when you will need to forgive and let go. Learn to experience what letting go feels like by trying the exercises in this chapter. Remember to communicate forgiveness. You may feel remorse, in which case don't turn your back on it. Let that person (even if it's you!) know that you have seen your own vulnerability and that you acknowledge the behaviour. Take a deep breath, stay calm and say 'I'm sorry, please forgive me, thank you, I love you.' Follow this with a hug. No-one is too young or too old to hear those words.

19

Going Back to Work

To make an end is to make a beginning.

T.S. Eliot

When you return to work can depend on where you live, your circumstances, whether you are in a salaried job or whether you are self-employed. It may be a choice, or it may not be a choice. Whenever it happens, it's the end of something and the beginning of something. It brings with it another change, another tumult of emotions, that you may be aware of consciously, or not. Even if you are happy and excited about going back to work it's not uncommon to have moments of worry and tearfulness.

Balancing a new routine and adding another thing to an already busy life as a new parent can have its ups and downs. I remember one occasion when I turned up to my job, suited and prepped for a big meeting, only for my CEO to point out that I had odd shoes on, in different colours.

> There have been times throughout the year where I longed to be back at work, nicely dressed with a hot coffee, having adult conversation. But, when the time came, I was both surprised and not surprised by how much sadness I had. However, I have really enjoyed this first week back at work, when I have

been busy enough in the hospital to be distracted. When thoughts would return to my son settling in at nursery my heart would hurt a little (a lot) and then the guilt and worry would sneak in. It is a transition for us all. I cannot think of another time in my life where there has been so much monumental change in such a short period of time. Affirmations that I have dotted around the house have helped with the overwhelming mix of feelings and emotions. My go-to affirmations have been: 'Inhale, exhale' and 'you are the woman you have always been, and more.'

Ruchi, mother to one child

Starting childcare

If you are going back to work, the day will arrive when you take your baby to childcare for the first time, or you welcome a childminder or nanny into your home. Or you might be preparing for a family member to look after your child. Throughout your baby's life there will be 'letting go moments' when their world grows a little bit bigger and their circle widens. Each time a letting go moment happens, you experience a form of separation. This happened when your baby was born, when you first gave them to someone else to hold, and when you first left them for a few hours. This will continue to happen; it will be school, then school trips. It's never easy but these letting go moments happen incrementally, so we can shift, adjust, shift and adjust as we go through life.

'Wherever you are, I am there.'

Tip: *If you can, start your child at day care, nursery, or with their childminder or nanny a couple of weeks before you go back, even if it's part-time. Test the routine out in the morning and use the time to tweak those routines so they run smoothly. Also use it as a time to gently transition into the next stage – this will benefit you and your baby.*

Walking away the first time you leave your child can be difficult, and you may feel a physical tug. This is your instinct lighting up; your need to protect your baby. Your brain will be working out: 'Can I trust this person?' 'Will my baby's needs be met?' I still feel that tug when my boys go away, and they are now teenagers. My mother calls it the invisible umbilical cord and says she even has it with me still. I love the idea that our family are all connected through this invisible web of love.

EXERCISE 48: THE INVISIBLE UMBILICAL CORD OF LOVE

This hypnosis visualisation can be soothing if you are separated from your baby for whatever reason. You are going to imagine your love seeking out and finding your baby. The more you do it the more effective it can be.

You can also talk to your child, even as a baby, about this invisible connection; they may be able to use it to soothe themselves as they get a little older.

1. Have your baby safely nearby. Close your eyes and just notice where they are. Notice the space that they are inhabiting. Notice how you can sense where they are even with your eyes closed. Now imagine a connection

from you to them, like an umbilical cord. The cord can run heart to navel or heart to heart – just allow what comes into you mind.

2. Put your hand on your heart and breathe into your heart, gathering love from every part of your body like a golden light, and then moving all that love through your heart.

3. Now imagine this golden, soothing, loving light cascading through the invisible umbilical cord. Imagine that golden light of love moving through, sparkling with love and warmth, all the way to your baby. Imagine that golden light of love moving through into your baby's body and into your baby's heart.

4. You can use this visualisation whenever you are near, or apart from, your child.

> **Tip:** *You can add a scent, like an essential oil, to this exercise to create a positive association that you can benefit from wherever you are. The more you practise this visualisation, with the smell nearby, the stronger the connection will be. Once, you've practised it often you could just have the scent on your wrist or on a small piece of cloth. Each time you smell it you will feel comforted and connected.*

Settling into work again

There are many advantages to being at work: opportunities for time on your own, to drink a hot cup of tea, and to eat lunch uninterrupted. Amazing! See those as moments for self-care. It may be tempting to work through your lunch break so you can leave for home earlier, or so you can get through your 'to do' list, but instead, use that time to rest and recharge your mind and body. Go out for some fresh air, eat a nutritious lunch, chat to a friend. And get away from your desk!

> Working part-time helped give me a day to myself where I could be me and feel good about myself in a work capacity, as it can be easy to get lost in the label of 'so and so's mummy'.
>
> *Kimberley, mother to two children*

Tip: *Add these moments of self-care to your gratitude jar (see page 38), such as: 'I ate lunch uninterrupted'. Small wins!*

Leaving stress at work

If you are allowing stress to build up at work, it can impact on how you feel when you head home and pick up your child. Finding ways to reduce stress and anxiety while at work will have a positive impact when you go home. Get into the habit of checking in with yourself throughout the day and noticing your feelings. Take moments throughout the day to bring yourself back into balance, and this will help your wellbeing.

You can do this by using your **Calm Breath**, and the Name it to Tame it exercise on page 248.

Challenges at work may include expressing or pumping. Many workplaces don't accommodate women who are breastfeeding, and it can be hard to express in a place where you don't feel safe and secure. If this is something you want to do, make use of visualisations to help. Remember that when you imagine something in detail in your mind, it can trigger physical responses in your body.

1. **Imagine:** Use a visualisation such as the milk dial from page 164.
2. **Listen:** Relaxing music is proven to help so get a play-list going so you have a few tracks to listen to on your phone.
3. **Affirm:** Remember why you are doing this and have an affirmation to help. 'I relax and allow my body to connect with the mother in me so I can nourish my baby.'

Being able to say no at work is of tremendous importance. Everybody will have different boundaries and be able to multi-task in different ways. When you are being asked to do more than is necessary within the timescale given, be aware

> **Tip:** *Go outside and get some fresh air every day, even if it is just walking or cycling to work, rather than getting the bus or tube. If you like, go to the gym, do yoga or go for a swim during your lunch break. Doing some exercise will get those endorphins moving, which will help to reduce stress, and make you more alert for work too.*

of the potential impact on you and your family. There are times when you will have to say 'no', when you may have said 'yes' in the past. This is mastering the art of the unapologetic no and it's okay! Each time you do this you are sticking to the terms of your contract, and protecting the precious time you have with your family. If you need a confidence boost to do this, try this affirmation:

> 'I breathe in and say no, I breathe out and let go.'

> If I was to have any sort of work – life balance and be out of the door at 5.30pm I had to say no. I quickly learned that if I said no, there was always someone willing to say yes, and the job would be done.
>
> *Liza, mother to two children*

EXERCISE 49: A MINDFUL MINUTE AT WORK

Another tool you can use when you return to work is a 'mindful minute'. Research shows that regular mindfulness moments woven into your day can make you more creative and productive. There are apps you can download that remind you to take your mindful minute, or you can just train yourself to stop for a minute every now and again through-out your day. None of your colleagues will even be aware that you are doing this! You can even do it in meetings if you feel your mind wandering.

- Take a deep breath.
- Bring your focus into your body. You can keep your eyes open or close them if you are able.

- Breathe out.
- Pause.
- Repeat the above, and keep going for one minute.

> **Tip:** *To keep motivated at work, and to help with efficiency, use the hypnosis tool for setting goals (see pages 45-8). You can use it for mini-goals and also short-, medium- and long-term project and career goals. You can also use the mini-goals visualisation (see page 118) to rehearse seeing a project finished, meetings with clients or colleagues, and prepare for an interview.*

After work

If you are at work, the time you have with your baby will be reduced. Taking time to really be present in the moments when you are together will be of huge benefit to you and to your child. When you leave work, shut the door on work.

> 'As I close the door behind me I shut work away.'

If you walk to work, even for just a short distance, do a mindful walk (see page 143) as part of your journey home as this can help you to leave work behind. If you are driving, when it is safe to do so (say, at every red light) say:

> 'Breathing in I am here, I am present, breathing out I let go of the day.'

You can do this quite easily on public transport too; maybe put that phone away and let your mind rest instead.

Just before you pick baby up or arrive home, stop and take a deep **Calm Breath**. Soften your shoulders, soften your hands and smile.

'As I let go of the day's work, I greet my baby with a smile.'

If you can, turn your phone off and ease into the evening routine with your baby. Nothing is more important than this moment. When you give your child a bath, or put them to bed, notice the details. Use exercises like the Breath-Baby-Connect on page 97, A Window to your Baby's Soul (see page 99), or, when you are feeding them, the Face-to-face Scan from page 166. Smile at your baby, be with them. What matters is the time you spend with them, doing what you can to make this good quality time, full of love, warmth and connection.

Summary

Prepare for your return to work as best you can. Use the techniques in the book to take opportunities to bring yourself into balance. Let go of work when you leave and turn your attention to your baby with soft shoulders, soft hands and a smile. And don't forget mastering the art of the unapologetic no.

20

Honouring your Journey

I may not have gone where I intended to go,
but I think I have ended up where I needed to be.

Douglas Adams

As the end of the first year comes around, feelings that
arise may take you by surprise. Glancing back over the
first year, you may remember your baby in your arms as you
held them for the first time. They seemed so tiny and fragile.
You may still be tired, but less tired than you were, and more
able to respond to the challenges that are thrown at you.
This is really important to remember; in the first year you
have learned many of the skills that will carry you through
the years to come.

'I celebrate our journey through the first year.'

Humans are complex beings and we are able to hold
and experience many emotions simultaneously, that's
the 'overwhelm'. I've learned a lot about myself this
past year and a big lesson has been making time
for self-care. It's something that I didn't have to pay
much deliberate attention to before having my son,
as in my pre-baby life I naturally did many things that

emotionally nourished me. However, that bank of resilience became depleted fairly quickly post-baby and I have learned that planning self-care is essential. The 'self-care' bit is a funny term as I have needed my village (my family and friends) to support me to take time to myself; someone has got to hold the baby! There's what I call the self-care: affirmations, mindfulness, music and naps when baby naps etc. Then there are the self-care activities, from a coffee in the garden, dinner and cinema date with my husband, an evening learning to brush letters, to a day spa and catch-ups with besties; all of these identity-affirming activities have only been possible because of my village, to whom I am forever grateful.

Ruchi, mother and clinical psychologist
(as well as many other things!)

Embracing the changes

Much has changed, and you have come a long way in a short space of time. You've grown into the mother you are now and, equipped with all the new knowledge you have learned, you have successfully navigated the ups and downs that the first year threw at you. You did it!

The connection with, and love for, your baby may have been instant, or it may have grown over the year. As you see their little character emerging, you may wonder who this little person is becoming, who they will be, what they will do, and what their interests will be. The truth is your children are never exactly how you expect them to be; they are their own independent, perfectly unique blend of environment and genetics, and as you watch them grow in the years to come you will become more used to the ebb and flow of parental feelings.

'Every day I am honouring myself and the feelings that arise.'

Your memories of the first year may be a blur of those early days, there may be a sense of sorrow and of time passing so quickly, but also a sense of relief that you made it! Remember the slow but fast stage I mentioned at the beginning of the book (see page 76)? Time seems to go slowly on some days, but suddenly, as this milestone is reached, it may feel as if it has gone so fast. This is the nature of parenting, and this is why being engaged and present in moments, as much as you can, is valuable in the long term. When you are in each moment as much as you can be, you experience what is real in each moment. You will be able to truly connect with your baby as they grow into each new stage. **PRESS PAUSE.**

'I love seeing you grow into the person you are now.'

Looking back to the birth

As your baby's birthday approaches you may want to reflect on their birth as well. As you move forward, you may also reflect back: 'This time last year I was … ' If your baby's birth was positive and you have positive memories this will be a comfortable and happy process. If you didn't have a totally positive experience of birth, you may find that feelings begin to bubble up in the days before your baby's first birthday. If you had a traumatic experience and find yourself unexpectedly struggling with this milestone, this may be a time to consider talking to your GP or health visitor, especially if you didn't before.

If you find yourself feeling anxious around this time, and if you have feelings of being overwhelmed, you can do exercises like the ladder breathing on page 126 or the sensory spotlight grounding exercise on page 123.

It can be helpful to think of your baby's birthday and your experience of birth as two separate things. It's okay to acknowledge how you feel about the birth on that date, but also to celebrate your baby's milestone.

EXERCISE 50: HONOURING YOUR PARTNER'S AND FAMILY'S JOURNEY

Often in the first year, the attention and focus is all on the mother. But a mother and baby also need the support of those around them, including the partner, who has been on their own transformational parenting journey. There may also be friends or family who have made meaningful contributions in the first year. Acknowledging and recognising that can be a meaningful way to strengthen the bond and connections within your family and your circle of support. You can do this exercise for as many people as you wish:

- Take a few moments to reflect on your partner/family/friend's support. Think about the moments that mattered; they may be small, they may be big.
- Write a note to them, acknowledging the support from them in a way that is personal to you.
- Give the note to your partner/family member/friend on your baby's first birthday.

EXERCISE 51: HONOURING YOUR JOURNEY

Reaching the one-year milestone is about so much more than a party and gifts for baby. It should also be an opportunity to honour what you have achieved. Your journey to this moment may have been smooth, or it may have been challenging. You may have had things to overcome; some things about becoming a mother may have been easier than others.

The first birthday of your baby is also the first birthday of the mother who has emerged from within you. Honour this part of you. Celebrate yourself and congratulate what you have done, because you are **incredible**. Look what you have achieved despite all the challenges that were thrown at you. You have loved, and cried, you may have held sorrow in your heart, and your heart may have almost exploded with joy. **You are amazing.**

What are you going to do to honour yourself? To recognise what you have done?

🎧 Honouring your Journey

This short visualisation is about honouring the mother in you. This track is available to download (see page 8). It's more powerful to listen to it, but you can read this shortened version out to yourself if you like. When listening, you may cry, but that's okay – remember your heart-opening tears (see page 113). These tears represent the fullness of life and are an expression of the wide-ranging emotions that arise as a mother. Listen to this track at any time you want to connect and see the whole mother in you.

1. When you are ready, make yourself comfortable, either lying down or sitting on a chair, with both feet on the ground.

2. Connect with your **Calm Breath** and sink into the rhythm of your breath. Imagine a golden light around you. With the next breath connect with every part of you, breathing in that golden light. Breathe it in and then move that breath down through your body into your heart, filling it with that golden light. This is a moment to just be, with an open heart.

3. Accept how you feel in this moment, acknowledge the mother in you and smile. Put your left hand on your heart and say to yourself:

'Thank you for everything you have felt and everything you have done.

Thank you for your sacrifices.
Thank you for your patience.
Thank you for your love.
Thank you for your guilt.
Thank you for your joy, your frustration, your sadness and your happiness.
Thank you for everything you have done, to arrive at this moment.
Thank you for all that you have been, all that you are right now, and all that you will be.'

1. Take as long as you need to sit in this feeling.
2. Imagine receiving a hug, a warm, gathering hug.
3. Breathe in deeply and then breathe out. Say to yourself: 'I will love and support you on this journey.' If you like, record this in your own voice and listen to it.

EXERCISE 52: A YEAR OF GRATITUDE

This book is rounded off with the gratitude exercise mentioned in the first part of the book. Remember your gratitude jar? Why not take a moment to empty it now, at the end of the year, and in your journal or a scrap-book, create a collage of mini-memories. Enjoy reading it to yourself, and maybe spend time making the collage with your child/ren and partner. If you like, add new affirmations, quotes and messages that remind you of what a transformative year it has been. From bump to baby: your little family unit, bound together through love, kindness and strength from now, through all the years to come.

Summary

How are you going to honour your journey? Look back and realise how far you have come and how much you have done. Parenting is an ever-evolving journey and learning to take each moment as it comes is a habit that will serve you well. Take everything you have learned from the last year into what lies ahead. There will still be tough days, there will be incredible days, and all the days in between. Enjoy the ride, take downtime when you need it and be kind to yourself. **PRESS PAUSE.**

Further Resources

Breastfeeding

The Womanly Art of Breastfeeding, La Leche League
The Positive Breastfeeding Book, Amy Brown
La Leche (laleche.org.uk)

Perinatal Mental Health

Why Perinatal Depression Matters, Mia Scotland
Why Birth Trauma Matters, Emma Svanberg
PANDAS (pandasfoundation.org.uk)
AIMS (aims.org.uk)
Maternal Journal (Maternaljournal.org.uk)
Make Birth Better (Birthbetter.org.uk)

Wellbeing and Mindfulness

Everyday Blessings: Mindfulness for Parents, Jon Kabat-Zinn
Pebble in My Pocket, Thich Nhat Hanh
Stand Tall Like a Mountain, Suzy Reading

Parenting Support

Gentle Parenting, Sarah Ockwell-Smith
The Whole-Brained Child, Dan Siegal
What Mothers Do, Naomi Stadlen
Why Mothering Matters, Maddie McMahon

Acknowledgements

A book isn't written by just one person, it's written by many
– especially in this case where so many of you have kindly
shared your stories and given input. Thank you to: My ever-
patient husband Gordon, for his unwavering support and
cups of tea. My mother Jenny for her insight and nourishment – both mind and stomach! Marjorie for being there
when I need her. To Katie Beere and Debbs Bennett, 'mothers
of boys', for being the best friends and keeping me afloat. As
always Mia Scotland for being there these last 12 years – you
are a huge part of this journey. To all the Mindful Mamma
teachers, especially Sue Henderson, Lola Wild, Jenny
Parsons, Ruchi Bashi and Holly Dawson for reading! Also,
thanks to Hannah Harding, Laura Allenby, Lorna Hayward.
The awesome Michele Donnison for making sense of my
doodles/squiggles and forgiving me for the disappearing
teaspoons. Julia Kellaway – a big thanks for being in the right
place at the right time, again! To my brilliant agent Jane
Graham-Maw, for her wisdom, guidance and patience … lots
of patience. Sam Jackson, my superb editor/book doula at
Vermilion, who always pushes me to be the best writer I can
be, and to Becky Alexander who miraculously made the
editing stage feel a breeze. Finally, to Finlay and Rory, the
wisest teachers of all, without whom I wouldn't have been
able to write this.

Index

Also available by Sophie Fletcher

Hypnosis and Mindfulness
Techniques for a Calm and
Confident Birth

mindful
hypnobirthing

SOPHIE FLETCHER

revised
and
updated

Feel relaxed and empowered
throughout the birth of your baby

In this bestselling birth book, hypnotherapist and doula Sophie Fletcher shares the secrets to having a safe and positive birth experience. Using powerful mindfulness and hypnosis techniques, relaxing MP3 tracks and inspiring birth stories, Sophie will help you:

· Use your mind and body together to stay focused and in control
· Draw on visualisation and breathing techniques to help birth progress
· Feel positive and empowered before, during and after you give birth

Reassuring, practical and based entirely on what works, *Mindful Hypnobirthing* is your essential guide to having a calm and confident birth.